Materiality and Subject in Marxism, (Post-)Structuralism, and Material Semiotics

Johannes Beetz

Materiality and Subject in Marxism, (Post-)Structuralism, and Material Semiotics

palgrave
macmillan

Johannes Beetz
University of Warwick
Coventry, West Midlands, United Kingdom

ISBN 978-1-137-59836-3   ISBN 978-1-137-59837-0   (eBook)
DOI 10.1057/978-1-137-59837-0

Library of Congress Control Number: 2016948588

Cover illustration: © Andrew Taylor/Flickr

Printed on acid-free paper

This Palgrave Macmillan imprint is published by Springer Nature
The registered company is Macmillan Publishers Ltd. London

I dedicate this book to Rolf and Elke

Acknowledgements

I would like to acknowledge the help I received from my friends when first working on the manuscript for this book. Luis Caballero, Stefan Diehl, Peter Dausend, Kara Kosciuch, Benedikt Schreiber, David Waldecker, and others all gave immensely helpful comments. I thank Veit Schwab and an anonymous reviewer for their many helpful suggestions in the last stages of writing. I also sincerely thank Chloe Fitzsimmons and Esme Chapman at Palgrave.

This book is based on a thesis written in the Department of Sociology at the Johannes Gutenberg-University in Mainz under the supervision of Johannes Angermuller, Stefan Hirschauer, and Michael Liegl. I thank them for their great supervision and comments. I am grateful for the ongoing supervision at the University of Warwick by Johannes Angermuller, whom I further thank for his help and support.

My deepest thanks go to my sister and friend Mareike Beetz for all her support, Georg Kolbeck for the wordplays, Palscal Ludwig for the sleepless nights, Broder Petersen for being an optimist, and especially to the amazing Marie Juin for everything.

CONTENTS

LIST OF FIGURES

CHAPTER 1

Introduction

Abstract The subject today seems decentered in and by language, split by
the unconscious, deformed by social forces, governed by ideology, and is
either seen to have succumbed to the postmodern condition or to never
have existed in the first place. Neither idealist philosophies nor new materialist approaches have adequately addressed the relation between subject
and materiality. Every materialist theory of the subject depends on a conception of materiality, which can delineate the character of what the material reality that the subject is constituted in consists of. This book offers
readings of the approaches of Marxism, (post-)structuralism, and material
semiotics and explores the relations between materiality and the subject in
each approach.

Keywords Marxism • (Post-)Structuralism • Material semiotics • Subject
• Materiality • Materialism

The rumor of the death of the subject has been spread for several decades
now. Every so often obituaries appear, proclaiming its demise. It is presented by theorists as decentered in and by language, split by the unconscious, deformed by social forces, governed by ideology, and seen either
to have succumbed to the postmodern condition or to never have existed
in the first place. In *The Ticklish Subject*, Slavoj Žižek writes that in the
Western social sciences and humanities there seems to be a wide consensus
concerning the rejection of the traditional concept of the subject (cf. Žižek

© The Author(s) 2016   1
J. Beetz, *Materiality and Subject in Marxism, (Post-)Structuralism,
and Material Semiotics*, DOI 10.1057/978-1-137-59837-0_1

2000, p. 1). This consensus, reaching from sociology, linguistics, and philosophy to literary theory and cultural studies, in a large part rests on a simplified rejection of what is almost interchangeably called the idealist, the Cartesian, the autonomous, or the bourgeois subject.

Descartes's self-transparent thinking subject, which dominated the Western understanding of subjectivity for almost 300 years after the publication of the *Meditations*, constitutes itself in the immaterial realm of the ideal. This ideational reality stands in opposition to the material world, which is of an entirely different ontological order. The dichotomies of material/immaterial as well as subject/object lie at the core of the idealist conception of the subject. What makes the Cartesian model an idealist one is its insistence on the primacy of the immaterial and ideal. The contemporary dissatisfaction with the Cartesian model and other idealist theories is, in many ways, well founded. Unsurprisingly, these idealisms have not been able to satisfyingly address and explicate the relation between subject and object, since they largely simply exclude material instances from their theories of the subject. What is more surprising and troubling, however, is that more recent scholarship, decidedly concerned with 'materiality' and a renewal of materialism, has not addressed the subject and its relation to 'matter' or materiality adequately either.

In materialist philosophy and theory the material takes primacy over the ideal. Therefore it can rely neither on the Cartesian *Cogito* nor on other idealist philosophies of the subject derived from it. The subject can consequently not be conceived of as an original, immaterial, and autonomous entity; rather it should be taken to be an effect, a process, or an endpoint, constituted in and by material reality. In this apparent inversion of idealism, the *material* now becomes the instance in which the subject is constituted. What this 'material' denotes is of central importance for the reach and explanatory power of materialism. Every materialist theory of the subject thus depends on a conception of *materiality*, which can delineate the character of what material reality consists of.

Only in the past few decades has *materiality* emerged as a field of study, crossing disciplinary boundaries and providing novel perspectives on social and cultural phenomena. The recently developing fields of *material culture studies*,[1] as well as what is called *New Materialism*,[2] encompass a multiplicity of approaches to various elements of the material world. In the social sciences and humanities the general increase in research concerned with material objects and materiality has been described as a 'material turn' (cf. e.g. Bennett and Joyce 2010). What, not long ago, was still considered as irreconcilable with the social and cultural is now studied as a part and sometimes an expression of the latter. The multitude of papers and books published on the topic of *materiality* can by no means be said to constitute a field of research representing a homogenous theory or a common definition of what is to be included in the study of the 'material.'

However, many of them appear, despite their heterogeneity, to be united in an eerie preoccupation with 'things' and 'matter' and in a surprisingly persistent exclusion of certain fundamental kinds of materiality. This is, at least partly, due to a pervasive understanding of materiality which not infrequently reverts to a reductionist materialism by restricting materiality to matter or matter in motion. This notion, then, conceives of material entities either as passive *objects* waiting to be acted upon and manipulated, or alternatively as exerting a persistent effectivity, agency, or vitality of some sort. In the first case, material entities are sometimes regarded as *materializations* of the immaterial or ideational (like 'culture,' social relations, or identity). In the other extreme, as a persistent and effective part of reality, they impose themselves as extra-cultural and extra-social forces. Regarding the material as just one, albeit privileged, realm of existence while retaining the ideational in the form of 'culture,' 'the subject,' 'language' or 'thought' simply inverts idealism without abandoning its dichotomous categories. Furthermore, approaches to materiality that limit their inquiries to phenomena that consist of matter necessarily exclude modalities of materiality not readily identifiable as tangible, solid or given.

Jane Bennett, to take just one prominent proponent of New Materialism, is predominantly concerned with the 'vital materiality' of 'lively things' and the '*vibrant matter*' that gave one of her books its name (Bennett 2010b, pp. vii–viii). Such a post-Deleuzian, self-described 'thing-power materialism' (Bennett 2010a, p. 47) neither adheres to the old dichotomies of subject and object, nor does it talk of things as being comprised of simple, passive matter. Rather, it grants them a vitality which, in a sense, allows the things to act. 'Agency' is shared, or distributed, between human and non-human actors. The occupation with different aspects of and entities in the material world, and their role in social practices and the social in general as well as in the formation of subjectivity, is no doubt justified and even crucial, it will be argued later. The fact, however, that Bennett and others discuss materiality in a way that favors matter and things, while enchanting the two with vitality and vibrancy,

makes intelligible the accusation that they posit 'matter against materialism' (Noys 2015)—and particularly against the historical, discursive, and
dialectical kinds.

Even though in Bennett's influential book the 'topic of subjectivity…
gets short shrift' (Bennett 2010b, p. ix)—which is certainly no coincidence—it can be said that many of the 'flat ontologies' and 'thing-
oriented' philosophies in her general proximity, while rejecting the
Cartesian subject, reduce subjectivity to agency and affect disseminated
in assemblages of human and non-human actors without developing a
theory of (what takes the place of) the subject or accounting for its constitution and decentering.[3] The opposite, namely retaining the notion of
an autonomous, centered subject that is the source and origin of social
practice and intentional activity, is by no means a viable alternative, as we
will see. The 'free' subject of classical humanism; the intentional actor
of some interactionist sociologies; the rational individual of economics;
or the subject as fount of transparent original meaning, that lives on in
some divisions of hermeneutics—none of these are suitable for a materialist approach to the subject, either. Thus, we will have to look somewhere
else. I suggest turning to some slightly 'older'—dialectical, historical,
discursive, semiotic—materialisms to help us work through the relation
between materiality and the subject. The last turn in the social sciences
and humanities (the 'material' one) might have been a wrong turn—if
only in the sense that it left some crucial things behind.

This book offers readings of the approaches of Marxism, (post-)struc-
turalism, and material semiotics and presents the three as contributing
in different ways to something like a non-reductionist 'materialism without matter,' to use Balibar's term (2007, p. 23). This does not entail
disregarding the importance of material 'objects' and 'things.' Rather, it
highlights a dissociation from reductive materialisms of matter and underlines the claim that materiality is multiple, complex, and not reducible
to tangible matter. In such a materialism, the subject is seen as an effect
of material conditions, relations, processes, and practices. The relation
between materiality and the subject as well as the mechanisms by and
through which the subject is constituted in this relation comprise the second focus of our investigation. Thus, this short monograph establishes
some characteristics of a non-reductionist materialism, which in turn
constitutes the basis for a materialist theory of the subject that does not
exhaust itself in a mere rejection of the Cartesian subject.

This book consists of five parts. Chapter 2 provides a brief philosophical prelude to what follows. It takes the Cartesian subject as well as its relation to the material world, the *res extensa*, as its point of departure as they serve as a background before which other conceptualizations of subjectivity can be characterized. To further grasp the idealist conception of the subject, Kant's transcendental idealism as well as Hegel's absolute idealism are discussed in regard to their respective conceptualization of subjectivity and materiality. It will be argued that the problem of the relation between the (immaterial) subject and material reality played a constitutive role for the philosophies designated as German idealism.

In the second part (Chap. 3) we will engage with Marx's materialism. The reading of Marx proposed here counters characterizations of Marxism as a deterministic, mechanistic, or economistic materialism in which subjects and their ideas are directly and univocally determined by the conditions they find themselves in. The chapter explores the multifarious materiality of *material conditions* as well as its relation to the ideological subject constituted in it. To this end central aspects of historical materialism are introduced and three notions of ideology implicit in Marx's work are identified and critically evaluated. It will be suggested that materiality appears in different, albeit interrelated modalities, none of which correlate with passive matter, and that the subject is constituted in these materialities.

Although Marxian theory offers a sound foundation for a non-reductionist materialism and a materialist theory of the subject, it will be maintained that the concepts of modes of production and ideology need revision. Chapter 4 introduces Louis Althusser's and Fredric Jameson's Marxisms as necessary extensions to classical Marxism which allow us to further determine the exact mechanisms and the kind of effectivity by which material conditions, as modes of production, condition the subject. The first part of the chapter revises the edificial model of base and superstructure and further refines the understanding of the concept of modes of production by arguing that it should not be restricted to the narrowly defined economic. The second part deals with Althusser's theory of ideology as it is found in his seminal text *Ideology and Ideological State Apparatuses* (Althusser 1972). Here, the subject appears as an effect of material ideological practices. The chapter closes with a typology of the different modalities of materiality encountered in Chaps. 3 and 4.

Chapter 5 turns to those approaches inspired by Saussurean semiotics, Marxism, and psychoanalysis commonly referred to as (post-)structuralism. Focusing on the materiality of language and discourse and its relation to the subject, this part in a first step introduces Saussure's structural linguistics and characterizes the heterogeneous assemblage of authors, such as Derrida, Lacan, Kristeva, Foucault, and others often subsumed under the label of '(post-)structuralists.' That language is presented as fundamentally material has consequences for the status of the thinking and speaking subject. Thus, upon illustrating the ramifications of this conception of language, different approaches to the constitution of the subject in material discourse are discussed. Briefly returning to the concept of ideology and sketching out an enunciative-pragmatic approach to discourse analysis, the subject will be considered as the effect of discursive positioning practices. Finally, the modalities of materiality encountered throughout the chapter are recounted. Again, what we find is that these materialities are not simply composed of tangible matter. Rather, they rely on practices, on processes, and on certain types of effectivity or 'facticity.'

The last part (Chap. 6) is concerned with actor–network theory and certain approaches in its vicinity which can be subsumed under the designation of material semiotics. Dealing with writers such as Bruno Latour, Donna Haraway, and John Law, this chapter introduces a materiality of materialization and discusses the consequences of seeing the subject as an effect of rhizomatic material assemblages. Material semiotics regards materiality as well as the subject as semiotic, relational effects or 'endpoints.' As a set of largely empirical and methodological works, it could—very cautiously—be characterized as an 'empirical version of post-structuralism' (Law 2009, p. 145). An introduction to the key features of this approach is followed by a delineation of its methodological suspension of such dichotomies as immaterial/material, subject/object, or active/passive. The consequences this suspension has for the understanding of materiality and the subject, as well as its methodological and terminological implications, are then exemplified. A short conclusion (Chap. 7) recounts the findings and contextualizes them.

The survey character of this short volume means that neither a full-blown theory of the subject nor a comprehensive non-reductionist materialism will be developed here. Besides offering concise introductions to Marxism, (post-)structuralism, and material semiotics and presenting their approaches to materiality and the subject, however, what follows can be seen as an intervention into the ongoing debates revolving around subjectivity and materiality in the social sciences and humanities. By reviewing and discussing the three approaches, I hope to contribute to an understanding of the subject and its constitution within the materiality of the social that encompasses not only tangible matter or matter in motion, but also the materiality of social relations, (ideological) practice, material processes, discourse, and the sometimes very material 'facticity' of the material conditions individuals find themselves in.

NOTES

1. See, e.g.: Graves-Brown (2000), Hicks and Beaudry (2010), Ingersoll (2008), and Miller (2005).
2. See, e.g.: De Landa (2009), Coole and Frost (2010), and Dolphijn and van der Tuin (2012).
3. There are, of course, important exceptions and the prominent inclusion of the material corporeal dimension in new materialist feminist theories of the subject, for instance, is one such example (cf. e.g. Dolphijn and van der Tuin (2012), pp. 158ff.).

REFERENCES

Althusser, L. (1972). Ideology and ideological state apparatuses (notes towards an investigation). In L. Althusser (Ed.), *Lenin and philosophy, and other essays* (pp. 127–188). New York: Monthly Review Press.

Balibar, E. (2007). *The philosophy of Marx.* London: Verso.

Bennett, J. (2010a). A vitalist stopover on the way to a new materialism. In D. H. Coole & S. Frost (Eds.), *New materialisms: Ontology, agency, and politics* (pp. 47–69). Durham, NC: Duke University Press.

Bennett, J. (2010b). *Vibrant matter: A political ecology of things.* Durham: Duke University Press.

Bennett, T., & Joyce, P. (2010). *Material powers: Cultural studies, history and the material turn.* London: Routledge.

Coole, D. H., & Frost, S. (Eds.). (2010). *New materialisms: Ontology, agency, and politics.* Durham, NC: Duke University Press.

De Landa, M. (2009). *A new philosophy of society: Assemblage theory and social complexity.* London: Continuum.

Dolphijn, R., & van der Tuin, I. (Eds.). (2012). *New materialism: Interviews and cartographies.* Ann Arbor: Open Humanities Press.

Graves-Brown, P. (Ed.). (2000). *Matter, materiality, and modern culture.* London: Routledge.

Hicks, D., & Beaudry, M. C. (Eds.). (2010). *The Oxford handbook of material culture studies.* Oxford: Oxford University Press.

Ingersoll, D. W., Jr., & Daniel, W. (2008). Material culture. In W. A. Darity (Ed.), *International encyclopedia of the social sciences* (pp. 12–18). Detroit: Macmillan Reference.

Law, J. (2009). Actor network theory and material semiotics. In B. S. Turner (Ed.), *The new Blackwell companion to social theory* (pp. 141–158). Chichester: Wiley-Blackwell.

Miller, D. (Ed.). (2005). *Materiality.* Durham, NC: Duke University Press.

Noys, B. (2015, October 27). Matter against materialism. Bruno Latour and the turn to objects. University of Warwick. Retrieved November 2, 2016, from https://www.academia.edu/21686931/Matter_against_Materialism_Bruno_Latour_and_the_Turn_to_Objects

Žižek, S. (2000). *The ticklish subject: The absent centre of political ontology.* London: Verso.

CHAPTER 2

Prelude: The Cartesian Subject
and German Idealism

Abstract The question of the relation between material reality and the immaterial subject has been a recurring theme in Western philosophy. This chapter introduces key features of the idealist philosophies of Descartes, Kant, and Hegel pertaining to the subject and its relation to the material world. All three are presented as giving primacy to the ideational, immaterial over the material. The Cartesian subject is introduced to serve as a background before which other conceptualizations of the subject can be characterized, and Kant's and Hegel's German idealism is summarized and their notions of subject and materiality explicated.

Keywords Descartes • Kant • Hegel • German idealism • Subject • Materiality

The subject is a strange thing. Mostly rejected as a workable category in the social sciences and humanities, the autonomous subject associated with Descartes's *Meditations* is criticized by literary theorists, cultural studies scholars, sociologists, linguists, and philosophers alike. At the same time, it keeps reappearing as a dangerous presence that is met with an almost reflexive dismissal. Žižek, who critiques, and in a way reasserts, the Cartesian subject from a Lacanian-Marxist perspective, calls it a *spectre* haunting Western academia (Žižek 2000, p. 1). Indeed, if we were to follow Derrida's characterization of quite a different spectre (that of Marx) as something 'as powerful as it is unreal, a hallucination or simulacrum that

© The Author(s) 2016
J. Beetz, *Materiality and Subject in Marxism, (Post-)Structuralism, and Material Semiotics*, DOI 10.1057/978-1-137-59837-0_2

is virtually more actual than what is so blithely called a living presence' (Derrida and Kamuf 2006, p. 13), there would certainly be a resemblance to the crasser representations of the free, self-contained subject. For the lack of its proponents it is not a living presence. It is hard to find even idealists who have a concept of the individual subject as autonomous and independent of *all* entities external to it, a subject, in short, that is pure *hypokmeímenon, subiectum*—foundation and origin—without being *subiectus*—subordinate, subjected (cf. Zima 2007, p. 3). In this sense, it does not have a proper reality outside of the polemic dissociations from it.[1] At the same time, it is powerful and actual by its continued latent informing of contemporary theories of the subject.

Unsurprisingly, René Descartes will here serve as the founding father of the classical model of subjectivity, which in turn will enable us to give a brief overview of the subject and its relation to the material world in German idealism. Briefly examining certain traits of Descartes's, Kant's, and Hegel's philosophies will introduce themes that continue to reappear throughout the discussion of the subject's relation to materiality. Such are the subject–object dichotomy; the mutual exclusivity of mind and matter; the self-awareness and autonomy of the thinking and acting subject; as well as the subject's relation to history and the social realm, to name just a few.

In his *Meditations on First Philosophy* (Descartes 1996), René Descartes, on his quest to establish 'one single indubitable fact from which all other truths could be determined' (Atkins 2005a, p. 8) by employing a method of doubt, comes to the conclusion that the only thing certain is that he thinks—that he is 'a thing that thinks' (Descartes 1996, p. 19). This thing that thinks, this 'being that thinking discovers as its support, is a totally autonomous being' (Negri 2007, p. 172, n. 166).

In a central passage of his second meditation Descartes writes: 'Thinking? At last I have discovered it - thought; this alone is inseparable from me. I am, I exist - that is certain. But for how long? For as long as I am thinking' (Descartes 1996, p. 18). Hence, the famous formula that stands at the center of Cartesian subjectivity - *cogito ergo sum*. This thinking thing, however, is peculiar in that it is *immaterial;* it is disjunct and ontologically distinct from matter, particularly from the body. Such substance dualism, the 'mutual exclusivity of matter (*res extensa*) and thought (*res cogitans*)' (Atkins , p. 2), still survives in theories of subjectivity today and serves as a reference point for contemporary discussions of subject–object dichotomy and the many attempts to overcome it (cf. e.g. Nancy 1991).

The subject that thinks and consciously knows that it is thinking presents itself as self-transparent. Thence, consciousness is knowable and controllable; the origin of intellect and the reasoning subject. The mind might be '[weak and] prone to error' (Descartes 1996, p. 21), but it can reflexively make itself aware of this weakness and by conscious effort eradicate it. There is no conscious part of the mind standing in the way of intellect and its capacity of self-knowledge; there are no divisions, no fractures, no fissures. If the aforementioned existed - and the 'I' was not identical with itself - they would be immediately perceivable (and God guarantees this fact).

If the *Cogito* is the only indisputable fact and if it is of a wholly different substance and belongs to a different realm of reality, then it, on the one hand, has primacy over the *res extensa* but cannot, on the other hand, be an active, involved part of this material reality, including the affection of the physical body. The reverse holds just as true: In Descartes, there is an emphasis, or 'a preference for the conscious processes of thought over every other impulse or sensation' (Mansfield 2000, pp. 14–15), derived from bodily organs like smell, pain, sight, or hearing, thereby making bodily afflictions of the mind a phenomenon of an antecedent order.

What the subject knows, then, - what has the *most reality* - are not the material things perceived by it, or the sensory perceptions that apprehend the things, but 'the ideas, or thoughts, of such things' (Descartes 1996, p. 24) that appear before its mind: ideas take precedence over material entities.

The Cartesian subject is autonomous because it is in control of its consciousness and is not determined by the material world, which belongs to a different ontological order, designated as *res extensa* by Descartes. For Descartes there does however exist an entity outside of the subject, which precedes the latter and is in a way necessitated by the impossibility of the subject creating itself out of nothing. For Descartes, this higher immaterial instance is God.

In regard to materiality and subjectivity, Descartes's Enlightenment philosophy can be presented in five main theses: (1) There is an insurmountable split between the material world (including the body) and the mind. (2) The immaterial mind has primacy over the (potentially unknowable and/or non-existent) material world outside the *Cogito*. (3) The thinking subject is an autonomous being that is conscious of its own existence. (4) The material world is accessible to natural sciences; everything else is subjectively tainted. (5) The subject is the center of moral, interest-driven, creative action.

Descarte's meditations ignited modern philosophical thought and exemplify Enlightenment thinking on the brink of skepticism. His doubt about the reality of the material world is halted only by a questionable move whereby he attempts to proof the existence of a subject-independent reality by invoking God—an immaterial entity not susceptible to rational inquiry. Equally, his rational naturalism, his reliance on the natural sciences and the faculty of criticism, bring him to the threshold of materialism: If logic and the newly emerging 'scientific method' hold the key to understanding the natural world, then where is the line to be drawn between explicable phenomena and inexplicable (autonomous) phenomena and processes? There seem to be only two options: a dualism of material entities governed by natural laws and immaterial entities belonging to another ontological order, on the one hand, or a mechanical materialism that reduces human subjects to robots governed by universal laws, on the other. Thus, two of the main problems of the Enlightenment were its constituent elements—rational criticism and scientific naturalism.

German idealism can, among many other things, be understood as an effort to rid the philosophies of the Enlightenment of the two consequences arising from their emphasis on rational criticism and scientific naturalism: rational criticism radicalized leads to skepticism, and scientific naturalism radicalized leads to materialism of one sort or another. As both of these consequences were unacceptable, alternatives had to be found to retain the faculties of criticism and naturalism without doubting everything or reducing all phenomena within reach to matter and motion (cf. Beiser 2000). In other words, German idealism set out to sustain the principles of the Enlightenment in the face of philosophical problems, which revolved around the relation between *materiality* and *subject*—namely between a material reality and the immaterial subject.

The subject in German idealism appears, first and foremost, as a self-contained, conscious and reflexive whole that is the origin and center of (perceived) reality. Its mind has philosophical primacy over the material world outside it. In fact, as the antithesis of the ideal, the material, i.e. sensual, is almost completely excluded from this conception of the subject (cf. Zima 2007, p. 97). This by no means implies that German idealism excluded the material world from philosophy altogether. As Frederick C. Beiser demonstrates in *German Idealism. The Struggle Against Subjectivism*, the idealists strove for a way out of skeptical subjectivism and therefore their undertaking can be understood as 'an attempt to prove the reality of the external world and to break out of the egocentric predicament' (Beiser 2002, p. viii).

Diverse and not seldom contradicting each other, the philosophical systems of Descartes and German idealists such as Fichte (ethical idealism), Kant (transcendental idealism), and Hegel (absolute idealism) still share fundamental features that justify grouping them together. They all share the idealist premise which states (1) the primacy of the immaterial over the material. Their common paradigm is that 'ideas (mental or spiritual entities) are primary and lie at the very foundation of reality, knowledge, and morality, while non-ideal entities (such as physical or material things) are secondary and perhaps even illusory' (Baur 2005, p. 1078). Following this division, they adhere to (2) a subject–object dichotomy, which could be said to lie at the core of another dichotomy: (3) the fundamental split between mind and body (and mind and nature); furthermore, they posit (4) a unity or indivisibility of the subject (be it empirical or transcendental); and finally, (5) the subject is deemed to be self-transparent, self-conscious and autonomous (from material determination), or at least potentially so.

Both Kant and Descartes placed the individual subject at the center of their philosophy (cf. e.g. Goldmann 1971, p. 26; Negri 2007) and thereby gave birth to the modern subject understood as a rational and responsible agent and bearer of rights. As Adorno points out, discussing the Cartesian subject poses the question of 'what exactly the topic of discussion should be… "Subject" can refer to the particular individual as well as to universal attributes of "consciousness in general"' (Adorno 1999, p. 245). While Descartes arrives at his *Cogito* as the only thing certain, in Kant's epistemology the individual person is the bearer of the transcendental subject that constitutes the objective world. This transcendental subject is the origin of reason as well as the *a priori* concepts of time, space and causality, without which understanding—and more importantly, the conceivability of the whole of nature and material reality—would not be possible. Although inherent in the empirical subject, the transcendental subject is *universal* and is said to be the human essence.[2] Whence the sometimes confusing identification of the Kantian subject with Reason, 'consciousness in general' (ibid.) or Humanity. The empirical subject, on the other hand, is an individual entity and comes closer to the Cartesian *Cogito*. While there is no room for a discussion in depth of these 'two distinct modes or forms of subject' (Azeri 2010, p. 271), we can highlight two aspects of Kant's philosophy pertaining to those forms and their relation to the realm of the material: one epistemological and one moral.

What lies at the center of Kant's epistemology is the refutation of Cartesian skepticism introduced above. In his *Critique of Pure Reason* (Kant 1996), Kant posits that we cannot know objects belonging to the material world *in themselves*. What we know of those things are *phenomenal representations* of them and not the *noumenal things-in-themselves*. The subject-innate, a priori categories of time and space are the *forms* of appearance of reality. Here, matter is reduced to '[w]hatever in an appearance corresponds to sensation' (ibid., p. 73). In other words,

> there would be no such thing as 'objects' for us if we did not make judgments applying our own a priori concepts (or categories) to the sensible manifold that is intuited by us through our own a priori forms of space and time. (Baur 2005, p. 1079)

In Kant's language, the appearances (the empirical objects of ordinary experience) are *empirically* real, but *transcendentally* ideal. In a nutshell, the material reality is real, but we cannot know it apart from our mental representations of it. The transcendental subject 'constructs the objective world out of an undifferentiated material' (Adorno 1999, p. 247).[3] Conversely, there is no subject without object. Epistemologically, the knowing subject depends on an object of knowledge; practically, every acting subject needs an object to act upon. Even the transcendental subject of German idealism needs the object world it constitutes to exist. This undifferentiated material that the subject relies upon to constitute the material reality resembles something like *materiality without form*.

The distinction between the noumenal and the phenomenal poses a question regarding the thinking subject. If the objects of our experience are appearances, there is something that *appears*, although what appears cannot be experienced *in itself*. Furthermore, the subject is also *afflicted* by those objects. Because the thinking self does not (and cannot), by inner or outer attendance, experience itself as an object like any other, it is not merely an appearance or a representation. The most we can say is that the transcendental subject is the consciousness of the existence of the empirical thinking subject (cf. Azeri 2010, p. 271), and for this consciousness the empirical subject is a 'highly unique and distinctive object of experience' (ibid.). At the same time, the subject exists in time and thus cannot be a thing-in-itself because time is an *a priori* category of intuition that has no conceptual validity for noumenal things. Kant's individual subject is not a physical entity, it is not a bodily subject, but something that takes a position between the phenomenal and the noumenal, while primarily being *ratio* rather than *physis* (cf. Zima 2007, pp. 97–98). Hence, in Kant we still find the dualism of mind and matter, albeit in a lesser form than in Descartes. As an immaterial *transcendental* subject that constructs the objective world, it necessarily precedes all experience (as well as all determination and effect, be it social, historical, physical, etc.) and is thereby a *precondition* to thinking. As an empirical subject that is afflicted by intuited objects in time and space, it still escapes the dichotomy of noumenal and phenomenal because it cannot be experienced as an object of intuition.

Epistemologically, all this leads Kant to a redefinition of knowledge and truth, that he himself likens to the Copernican revolution in astronomy (Kant 1996, p. 21). According to him, 'it ha[d] been assumed that all our cognition must conform to objects'; that, however, has 'come to nothing,' which is why he proposes to assume that 'objects must conform to our cognition' instead (ibid.).

That means, '[i]nstead of reality shaping knowledge, it is human judgment that should be read into so-called reality' (Azeri 2010, p. 270). Objects must conform to the a priori categories of time, space and causality, before they can be objects of knowledge. Thus, the subject constructs reality and the transcendental subject as origin of those a priori concepts is the precondition of any perception of the empirical subject.

The last point to make regarding Kant is one concerning his ethics and the question of subject autonomy. What does it mean for the subject, if, as Žižek rightfully proclaims, 'for Kant... the greatest moral good is to lead a fully autonomous life as a free rational agent, and the worst evil [is the] subjection to the will of another' (Žižek 2009, p. 95)? Surprisingly, leading a 'fully autonomous life' does not entail being fully autonomous, and being a 'free rational agent' does not imply being free from subjugation. Here, we find again the dialectics of the *subiectum/subiectus* introduced above. The subject of Kant's ethics is origin and foundation as well as subjected and subordinated. To be an autonomous agent, the subject has to subordinate themself to the universal moral law and Reason. A community of autonomous subjects, as the *telos*, depends, for Kant, on these subjugations, which are located in the ideational sphere and refer to morality and reason as universal essences. As Hall points out, 'there is no allowance in Kant that different material circumstances, cultural contexts, legacies, and/or language systems might create strikingly different moralities and universalities' (Hall 2004, p. 29).

Hegel, like Descartes and Kant, gives primacy to the ideational over the material. Nevertheless, he introduces novel elements to the philosophy of German idealism. For instance, rationality and reason, two key terms in Kant's considerations on subjectivity, mature, for Hegel, 'in a dialectical process that… reveals the development of reason's own capacities in various social and historical epochs' (Melamed and Thielke 2005, p. 976). Reason is historical in nature rather than a universal, unchangeable principle. The teleological character of Hegel's historicism reintroduces such a universal reason, under the guise of absolute Spirit (*Absoluter Geist*), as the endpoint of history; but at a particular stage of this 'development of reason's own capacities,' reason and the reasoning subject cannot go beyond their historical and social limitations.[4] The subject is not merely caught up in socio-historical conditions; it is also *constituted*, a thing that emerges from interacting with the world. Hegel recognizes that an individual's self-consciousness—the core of its subjectivity—never exists in isolation, rather 'it always exists in relationship to an "other" or "others" who serve to validate its existence' (Hall 2004, p. 51). This 'other' is, initially, an object ('no subject without object'). However, it needs to be something more to constitute a self-conscious subject: it needs to be a self-consciousness itself. Hegel writes that

> [s]elf-consciousness is, to begin with, simple being-for-self, self-equal through the exclusion from itself of everything else. For it, its essence and absolute object is 'I'; and in this immediacy, or in this [mere] being, of its being-for-self, it is an individual. What is 'other' for it is an unessential, negatively characterized object. But the 'other' is also a self-consciousness; one individual is confronted by another individual. (Hegel 1977, p. 113)

Human individuals are not born as subjects; they need an 'other' to *recognize* them as such to constitute themselves as subjects proper, as self-conscious individuals. There is no subject without object—but also no self-conscious subject without an objectified 'other' subject to recognize the self-consciousness of that subject. As demonstrated in the famous 'lordship and bondage' passage in his *Phenomenology of Spirit* (Hegel 1977), the relationship between two self-conscious entities, which depend on one another to constitute themselves as subjects, is fundamentally one of conflict and struggle. Essentially, the master needs the slave to recognize him as a self-conscious subject.[5] In order to become self-conscious, a being must be recognized and, in turn, recognize another self-consciousness. 'Self-consciousness exists in and for itself when, and by the fact that, it so exists for another; that is, it exists only in being acknowledged' (Hegel 1977, p. 111). Thus, the subject's self-relation is not understood as 'something that exists immediately, prior to participating in an intersubjective realm of language and action, but as something that emerges from this experience' (Bykova 2009, p. 268). This makes the emergence of self-conscious subjects a *social phenomenon*, i.e. it always depends on an other.

There is something at work behind both historical development and the constitution of subjects. While Descartes and Kant seek to extract eternal truths about being in the world, Hegel historicizes philosophy and the human condition. History is regarded as a progression towards an end, which is the absolute Spirit. Hegel writes: 'The History of the world is none other than the progress of the consciousness of freedom' (Hegel 2004, p. 19). This consciousness, the immaterial Spirit (*Geist*), is a totality that manifests itself in the material world and the individuals involved in it. Matter, as the antithesis of the idea, can only be understood here as the material manifestation of something immaterial; an immaterial idea, which has real priority over the material universe.

The unfolding of the Spirit is what really determines the world. The concept of Spirit encompasses the individual subject's life (as subjective spirit) as well as the communal spirit embodied in social formations (as objective spirit) (cf. Atkins 2005b, p. 60). The latter 'concrete and practical' side of this ideational, universal subject manifesting itself can then be understood as '*the historical peoples* as successive embodiments of the "world-spirit", i.e. the progress of civilization' (Balibar 2007, p. 26). That means, even though subjects are constituted, subjectivated, in the properly social instances of the mutual recognition of self-conscious individuals, what lies beneath and really drives these processes is the absolute Spirit, which remains in the ideational realm. Development and progress exist, as do historical changes in how humans think and act; but rather than mankind transforming itself and its world, it is the Spirit coming to itself, moving towards its teleological goal.

It can be said that the Spirit determines everything, including subjects. But what kind of determination do we find here? As an immaterial totality progressing in time towards an endpoint, it is not a mechanical determination through which actions of the Spirit find a direct correlation in the actions and thoughts of subjects. The relation between the immaterial Spirit (the idea) and the material *social* reality is an expressive relationship where the idea *expresses itself* as a totality in its elements. For Althusser, whose concept of *structural* causality will play an important role in our discussion of the relation between the subject and material conditions in the coming chapters, this expressive causality is one of two ways to think effectivity in classical philosophy.[6] This model of determination, which dominates Hegel's thought,

> presupposes in principle that the whole in question be reducible to an *inner essence,* of which the elements of the whole are then no more than the phenomenal forms of expression, the inner principle of the essence being present at each point in the whole, such that at each moment it is possible to write the immediately adequate equation: *such and such an element* (economic, political, legal, literary, religious, etc., in Hegel) = *the inner essence of the whole.* (Althusser and Balibar 1997, pp. 186–187)

Socio-historical conditions and their individuals express the inner essence of the unfolding whole at a stage in its development. There is a causal relation between the immaterial and the material, albeit an *expressive causality.*

There is, of course, much more to Hegel's absolute idealism—the whole dialectical character of his philosophy has been omitted here—but what can be asserted is that the idea has primacy and is the true source of changes in the (human) world and its organization. It is the idea that changes the world and not the material world that changes ideas. Even though Hegel's is an idealist system (he calls it *absolute* idealism!) it should be noted that the subject constitutes itself in *inter*subjective processes and that his philosophy recognizes the historicity of social formations. With the core principles of the Cartesian subject and German idealism introduced, we can now move on to Marxist materialism and its understanding of materiality and the subject as well as their relation.

NOTES

1. In recent theoretical interventions regarding the notion of the subject in post-modernity, the 'centered' Cartesian subject has served as an antidote to the decentered, fissured, and in some regards impotent subject that emerged with the rise of structuralism. Negri, Žižek, as well as Badiou have called for (different versions of) a return to Descartes (cf. Negri 2007; Badiou 2013; Žižek 2000; Zima 2007).

2. Foucault would later call this subject 'a strange empirico-transcendental doublet, since he is a being such that knowledge will be attained in him of what renders all knowledge possible' (Foucault 2002, p. 347).

3. Ascribing the world external to the thinking subject the status of empirical reality, while simultaneously emphasizing its transcendental ideality, resembles the characterization 'reality' will undergo in (post-)structuralist theories presented in Chap. 5. As Fredrick Jameson remarks, in semiological thought, for instance, the whole of reality becomes problematical and might appear as 'a formless chaos of which one cannot even speak in the first place' (Jameson 1974, p. 33). Similarly, Lacan uses the concept of the Real to indicate that there is something, which lies outside the Symbolic Order (cf. e.g. Fink 1995, p. 24).

4. And which is why, if we want to follow his own metaphysics, Hegel couldn't become Marx.

5. For a thorough and helpful commentary on this passage, see (e.g. Atkins 2005b).

6. The other one is mechanistic causality, which he describes as 'Cartesian in origin' (Althusser and Balibar 1997, p. 186).

REFERENCES

Adorno, T. W. (1999). *Critical models.* New York: Columbia University Press.

Althusser, L., & Balibar, E. (1997). *Reading Capital.* London: Verso.

Atkins, K. (2005a). Commentary on Descartes. In K. Atkins (Ed.), *Self and subjectivity* (pp. 7–11). Malden, MA: Blackwell Pub.

Atkins, K. (2005b). Commentary on Hegel. In K. Atkins (Ed.), *Self and subjectivity* (pp. 60–64). Malden, MA: Blackwell Pub.

Atkins, K. (Ed.). (2005c). *Self and subjectivity.* Malden, MA: Blackwell Pub.

Azeri, S. (2010). Transcendental subject vs. empirical self: On Kant's account of subjectivity. *Filozofia, 65*(3), 269–283.

Badiou, A. (2013). *Theory of the subject.* London: Bloomsbury Academic.

Balibar, E. (2007). *The philosophy of Marx.* London: Verso.

Baur, M. (2005). Idealism. In M. C. Horowitz (Ed.), *New dictionary of the history of ideas* (pp. 1078–1082). New York: Charles Scribner's Sons.

Beiser, F. (2000). The Enlightenment and idealism. In K. Ameriks (Ed.), *The Cambridge companion to German idealism* (pp. 18–36). Cambridge: Cambridge University Press.

Beiser, F. (2002). *German idealism: The struggle against subjectivism, 1781–1801.* Cambridge, MA: Harvard University Press.

Bykova, M. F. (2009). Spirit and concrete subjectivity in Hegel's 'phenomenology of spirit'. In K. R. Westphal (Ed.), *The Blackwell guide to Hegel's phenomenology of spirit* (pp. 265–295). Malden: Wiley-Blackwell.

Derrida, J., & Kamuf, P. (2006). *Specters of Marx: The state of the debt, the work of mourning and the new international.* New York: Routledge.

Descartes, R. (1996). *Meditations on first philosophy.* New York: Cambridge University Press.

Fink, B. (1995). *Subject, object, and other basic concepts of Lacanian psychoanalysis.* Princeton, NJ: Princeton University Press.

Foucault, M. (2002). *The order of things: An archaeology of the human sciences.* London: Routledge.

Goldmann, L. (1971). *Immanuel Kant.* London: NLB.

Hall, D. E. (2004). *Subjectivity.* New York: Routledge.

Hegel, G. W. F. (1977). *Phenomenology of spirit.* Oxford: Clarendon Press.

Hegel, G. W. F. (2004). *The philosophy of history.* Mineola, NY: Dover Publications.

Jameson, F. (1974). *The prison-house of language: A critical account of structuralism and Russian formalism.* Princeton, NJ: Princeton University Press.

Kant, I. (1996). *Critique of pure reason.* Indianapolis, IN: Hackett Pub.

Mansfield, N. (2000). *Subjectivity: Theories of the self from Freud to Haraway.* St Leonards, NSW: Allen & Unwin.

Melamed, Y. Y., & Thielke, P. (2005). Hegelianism. In M. C. Horowitz (Ed.), *New dictionary of the history of ideas* (pp. 975–977). New York: Charles Scribner's Sons.

Nancy, J.-L. (1991). Introduction. In E. Cadava, P. Connor, & J.-L. Nancy (Eds.), *Who comes after the subject?* (pp. 1–8). New York: Routledge.

Negri, A. (2007). *The political Descartes: Reason, ideology and the bourgeois project.* London: Verso.

Zima, P. V. (2007). *Theorie des Subjekts: Subjektivität und Identität zwischen Moderne und Postmoderne.* Tübingen, Basel: Francke.

Žižek, S. (2000). *The ticklish subject: The absent centre of political ontology.* London: Verso.

Žižek, S. (2009). Discipline between two freedoms—Madness and habit in German idealism. In M. Gabriel & S. Žižek (Eds.), *Mythology, madness, and laughter: Subjectivity in German idealism* (pp. 95–121). London: Continuum.

CHAPTER 3

The Materiality of Conditions
and the Subject of Ideology

Abstract In Marxism, it is the material conditions that constitute and form the subject. The subject that emerges in relation to material conditions is an ideological subject. The chapter gives a concise introduction to Marxian materialism, while delineating the kinds of materiality that make up material conditions and investigating how exactly these materialities condition, determine, or affect the subject. To this end historical materialism, the metaphor of base and superstructure, as well as three different notions of ideology which are implicit in Marx's writings are presented. Materiality is shown to be irreducible to physical, tangible matter and the subject should be seen as effect, rather than as starting point and origin of thought and action.

Keywords Marxism • Ideology • Materialism • Materiality • Subject • Material conditions

In a crossed-out section of a manuscript which was abandoned for almost a century to the 'gnawing criticism of the mice' (Marx 1999, p. 2) before being published as *The German Ideology* in 1932, Karl Marx and Frederick Engels write that '[a]ccording to the Hegelian system, ideas, thoughts, and concepts produced, determined, dominated the real life of men, their material world, their actual relations...' (Marx and Engels 1965, p. 24). It is this supposed determination of the material world by immaterial ideas that they set out to 'debunk and discredit' as a 'philosophic struggle with the shadows of reality' (ibid.). To the idealism presented in the last chapter, Marx and Engels juxtapose a materialism that begins with premises that are not abstract but concrete, namely 'the real individuals, their activity and the material conditions under which they live, both those which they find already existing and those produced by their activity' (ibid., p. 32). In this approach, it is no longer ideas that determine the material world, but the material world that determines subjects and their ideas. The first kind of materiality we encounter here is that of *material conditions*. In Marxian theory the materiality of material conditions does not merely consist of tangible matter but also of relations, practices, and processes. This amounts to the assertion that there are several modes of being material—several *modalities of materiality*.

The subject of this materialism is not constitutive of all reality but constituted in a material social reality that is the result of practical human activity. It is thus best described as an effect of material relations, processes, and practices. Marx himself produced neither a grand theory of the subject, nor is his notion of materiality made explicit in his writings. Rather, both remain implicit and scattered throughout his work. The aim of the present chapter, then, is twofold. First, it attempts to determine what exactly 'material conditions' denote in a *Marxian materialism*, and to specify their *materiality*. Second, it investigates how this materiality conditions, determines, or effects the subject.

The subject that emerges in relation to the material conditions is an *ideological subject*. The vagueness of the term *ideology* makes it necessary to ascertain the different meanings it takes in Marx's theory. To this end, three different notions of ideology that are implicit in his writings will be presented. In each notion the relation of the subject to its material conditions shifts. However, as will be shown, both Marx's theory of ideology and his implicit theory of the subject are incomplete and can benefit from the amendments and extensions provided to them by later Marxists.

Theses on Feuerbach and the German Ideology: Marx's Materialism

Materialism denotes, first and foremost, the primacy of the *material* over the *ideal* and thus stands opposed to *idealism*.[1] In this respect, materiality is a negative term that can preliminarily be defined as that which is *not* ideal or ideational. This minimal definition of materiality in Marxist materialism allows the specification of the material as the stuff that is independent of, or at least external to, consciousness. We have already seen that in German idealism the subject is not only centered and unified, but also the source of reality. This notion is now turned on its head and rotated to the left with material reality becoming a factor determining the subject. We need, however, to go a few steps further to get to the core of Marx's 'historical materialism,' simply because assuming the primacy of the material world over the immaterial ideational realm is something *all* materialisms have in common by definition.

Marx's theory emerged not only from a reversal of Hegelian idealism, but also from a distancing from prior, 'classical' materialisms—especially Feuerbach's. What he criticizes in Feuerbach is that the latter has a passive view on objects and our perceptions of them and that such a passive stance with regard to the (material) object world is unable to (re)solve *philosophical* problems. Marx intends to formulate a materialism that encompasses *practical human activity*. This aspect of his materialism will become a major building block of Marx's social theory. The inclusion of practical activity in materialism is accomplished by combining elements of Hegelian idealism with Feuerbachian materialism.[2]

The *Theses on Feuerbach* (Marx 2010), written by Marx in 1845 and posthumously published by Engels, can be seen as one of the birth certificates of Marxian materialism. Here, Marx mainly criticizes what could be called a *positivist* materialism. In the first thesis he writes that the 'chief defect of all previous materialism (that of Feuerbach included) is that things [*Gegenstand*], reality, sensuousness are conceived only in the form of the object, or of contemplation, but not as sensuous human activity, practice, not subjectively' (ibid., p. 3). In other words, material reality is merely an object of passive contemplation and observation and not of practical activity. To rid materialism of this weakness, Marx proposes an active subject that is not just conditioned by material reality but shapes the world it lives in. The material world cannot be understood as dissociated from human activity. Thus, its materiality should not be conceptualized as consisting of passive matter, but be seen as multiple and related to practice. The theses are thus simultaneously a critique of 'old materialism' and German idealism. Marx wants sensuousness understood as concrete human activity while rejecting idealism, which acknowledges this active side of sensuousness, but only does so abstractly.

The subject of idealist philosophy actively constitutes the material world. This subjective constitution is, however, a mental activity and not a practical, sensuous one.[3] Feuerbachian materialism, on the contrary, posits a subject that, because of its predominantly passive character, is determined by the material world without being actively involved in the production and change of this world. Such positivist materialism that conceives the world as explainable in terms of matter is a contemplative interpretation of reality that, in a way, merely substitutes the immaterial organizing principles of idealism (mind) with another principle (matter). For Marx, the whole point of materialism is to change the world, so Feuerbach's materialism has to be modified. But why does he make changing the world the main aim of his new materialism?

The famous 11th thesis—'The philosophers have only interpreted the world in various ways; the point is to change it' (Marx 2010, p. 5)—appears in a new light when it is understood as a call to unite theory and practice. Not in the sense that we should all stop reading, writing, and thinking and instead go out on the streets and start a revolution (which is how it has often been interpreted, and understandably so, considering the idea's appeal), but in the sense of 'the resolution of theoretical problems by practical activity' (Singer 2000, p. 43). One example of such a resolution touches epistemological questions introduced in the last chapter because the emphasis on practice also redefines 'objective' truth of human thinking as a practical, not a theoretical problem. The 2nd thesis reads: 'Man must prove the truth, i.e., the reality and power, the this-worldliness of his thinking in practice. The dispute over the reality or non-reality of thinking which is isolated from practice is a purely scholastic question' (Marx 2010, p. 3).

The unity of theory and practice must also (and foremost) be understood as the resolution of contradictions not through interpretation and thought, but by active change. Philosophical contradictions can be resolved only by changing the world in which these contradictions become apparent. The resolution of contradictions inherent in the world is reminiscent of Hegel's philosophy of history. There, contradictions are dialectically resolved and give birth to something new that is the synthesis of the contradicting elements (thesis and antithesis). But now, rather than thought (the idea, the Spirit), it is practical human activity that plays the crucial role in this dialectic. It is a materialist conception of history that sees the practical activity of humans and not some immaterial principle or entity as the driving force of world history and social reality.

The sensuous world (and especially nature) that the passive subject is confronted with in what Marx calls the 'old materialism,' is unchanging. In the materialist conception of history, the first traces of which we can find in the *Theses on Feuerbach*, this sensuous world is a product of history ('the result of the activity of a whole succession of generations, each standing on the shoulders of the preceding one' (Marx and Engels 1965, p. 57)), and tied to social systems that are in a constant flux and infused with contradictions. Consequently, Feuerbach's notion of 'man' is criticized as an abstraction that fails to see men and women as belonging to a particular social formation (cf. Marx and Engels 2010, p. 5). By acknowledging the historical and social situatedness of concrete men and women, any concept of human essence is either abandoned or radically remodeled into one of 'species being' because what men and women are results from their existing conditions of life. In *The German Ideology*, Marx and Engels give a more elaborate description of their historical materialism.[4] A polemic against Young Hegelians and 'old' materialists, the text introduces a materialist conception of history and an elaboration on the notion that it is material life or material conditions that can be utilized to understand history and (individual and collective) consciousness, and not the other way around, thereby famously reversing Hegelian idealism. In the afterword to the second edition of *Capital*, Marx writes that 'with [Hegel, the dialectic] is standing on its head. It must be turned right side up again, if you would discover the rational kernel within the mystical shell' (Marx 1990, p. 103). The mystical shell being the idealist premises and the rational kernel the dialectic.[5]

Marx and Engels give a historical account of the emergence and genesis of social forms that takes something quite banal as its starting point: 'the existence of living human individuals' (Marx and Engels 1965, p. 31). For there to be history, there must be humans. And being alive as a human involves eating, drinking, habitation, clothing and many other material things most of which cannot just be plucked from a tree or picked up from the ground. For Marx, what separates humans from animals is the fact that they produce the means to satisfy their needs, that is to say: produce their material life. This activity is the precondition of history altogether because '[t]he first historical act of these individuals distinguishing them from animals is not that they think, but that they begin to produce their means of subsistence' (ibid., p. 31 [crossed-out section in the original manuscript]). This production[6] can take on different forms depending on what is produced and how it is produced as well as the material conditions that individuals find already existing ('nature') or the ones that are produced by their activity (cf. ibid., p. 32).

In the collective production of their material life individuals use tools, machines, instruments, technologies, land, buildings, modes of transportation, available resources, and so on as means of labor. Together with human labor power (quite simply the capacity to work that workers have to sell, encompassing both practical knowledge and physical ability) they can be subsumed under the name of productive forces.

What means of labor are available and in use (the wheel, the steam engine, the iPad) is (relatively) specific to the stage in the development of those forces. According to the respective stage there are definite social relations that individuals enter into. Such relations include the (unequal) distribution of the means of production, the division of labor, property relations, and all other relations individuals enter in order to produce their material life. Not only in capitalism are these relations marked by exploitation, power, and dominance. They are independent of the wills of the individuals who inevitably enter them. Together with the material forces of production those relations of production form, in their historically particular combination, the mode of production, while the 'totality of these relations of production constitutes the economic structure of society' (Marx 1999, p. 2). The material reality of the respective mode of production, that is the way in which a society organizes the production of material life, is what—in the last instance—determines the way individuals think and act.

For Marx, different modes of production of material life equal different forms of consciousness and subjectivity and condition 'the general process of social, political and intellectual life. It is not the consciousness of men that determines their existence, but their social existence that determines their consciousness' (ibid.). The subject is no longer the origin and the center of reality. And neither does it remain in that other-worldly realm of ideas, principles, and abstractions. The material reality—the social and material conditions at a certain time in a certain place—constitutes 'subjects or forms of subjectivity and consciousness in the very field of objectivity. From its "transcendent" or "transcendental" position, subjectivity has shifted into a position of effect or result of the social process' (Balibar 2007, p. 66). Stripped of its metaphysical content, the subject is now devoid of its 'substance.' What had been conceived of by philosophers abstractly as 'man,' now finds its basis in the 'sum of productive forces, capital funds and social forms of intercourse, which every individual and generation finds in existence as something given' (Marx and Engels 1965, p. 50). The social processes and circumstances that exert their material force on the subjects they constitute are created (collectively) by individuals. Productive forces, for example, have no existence outside the infinite network of interacting, communicating and associating individuals. In bourgeois social formations they appear as something outside of and alien to those individuals because they experience themselves as isolated, individual subjects. This is a dialectic that other materialisms failed and fail to recognize, namely: 'that circumstances make men just as much as men make circumstances' (ibid.).

To better understand historical materialism and what it has to tell us about the relationship between materiality and the subject it is necessary to present a few points concerning the modes of production and their change throughout time. If the mode of production is 'the central organizing category of Marxism' (Jameson 2002, p. 18) and also presents the ultimately determining instance in the formation of subjects, it will be important to understand how modes of production develop and what their effect is. Furthermore, it will shed some more light on what kind of materiality it is that Marx has in mind when he writes about material life, material conditions, and the material world.

We have already established that the mode of production denotes a specific combination of productive forces and relations of production. Now we can add that productive forces and relations of production can come into conflict and contradict each other. This happens when the productive forces reach a point in their development (e.g. by means of technology or discovery) where the old forms of social organization become insufficient or obsolete and inhibit a production of material life that is appropriate to these advanced forces. The resolution of these contradictions finally takes place in the form of social revolutions. Obviously it is a little more complicated than this. But even in a mechanistic reading like this it is apparent that material forces and processes are the driving force behind history.[7]

In *The German Ideology* the succession of modes of production still seems like a relatively linear development in stages.[8] Quoting Fredric Jameson, we can enumerate these 'stages' of human society as

> primitive communism or tribal society (the horde), the gens or hierarchical kinship societies (Neolithic society), the Asiatic mode of production (so-called Oriental despotism), the polis or an oligarchic slaveholding society (the ancient mode of production), feudalism, capitalism, and communism (with a good deal of debate as to whether the 'transitional' stage between these last—sometimes called 'socialism'—is a genuine mode of production in its own right or not). (Jameson 2002, p. 75)

At each stage we find different forms of the division of labor, different property relations, and different modes of exchange. Without going into detail we can say that the specific constellation of all the elements of a mode of production constitutes the economic sphere of a given collective. As we will see in a moment, shifts in the organization of economic reality lead to or condition[9] changes in the ideological forms through which a social reality is represented. The difference between change in 'culture,' ideology, consciousness, subjectivity etc. and the 'material transformation of the economic conditions of production' is that the latter can, according to Marx, be 'determined with the precision of natural science' (Marx 1999, p. 2).

Indeed, this empirical or objective reality is one aspect of the materiality of economic conditions and might best be conceptualized as a materiality of effectivity or objectivity. Something like 'the distribution of means of production' is intangible in its materiality. Sure, there are factories built of stones, machines made of steel, material documents, computers, roads and railways all of which are made up of a positive materiality of matter ('things,' atoms, molecules); but the economic reality is not reducible to matter. Rather, the materiality of a mode of production refers not only to tangible 'hard' matter, but equally so to observable human activity; practices; processes; definite (i.e. objective) relations individuals enter with things and other individuals; forms of property; and so forth, which all have in common that they are (sensuously) real and do not exist for consciousness only. The 'material' of this approach comes closer to what we are left with after we discard all the 'idealist humbug' (Marx and Engels 1965, p. 50) and its immaterial but determining ideas.

Throughout history material conditions change and this change can be described as transformed economic conditions of production. In orthodox Marxism, the revolutions that bring about those transformations appear as necessary resolutions of real contradictions. History is seen as the progression of different modes of production that teleologically succeed one another. Each mode is then seen as a separate 'entity' with relatively specific and unique characteristics. According to this mechanistic view the stages introduced above can be presented as shown in Fig. 3.1).

As minimalistic as it may be, this figure illustrates some problems of the 'classical' notion of modes of production. What will interest us most are the bold lines separating the different forms of society. The lines are problematic because they suggest (1) that only one mode of production exists at a given time and that there is a definite break between the

Modes of Production

Primitive communism

Gens / Hierarchical kinship societies

Asiatic mode of production

Polis / slaveholding societies

Feudalism

Capitalism

[*Socialism*]

Communism

Fig. 3.1 Modes of production

different stages and (2) that there is a necessary progression towards an end (the last two modes are projected into the future). Although the illustration is both greatly simplified and exaggerated, it represents a persistent misinterpretation of Marx's writing.[10] The two problems mentioned above become particularly relevant if the material economic reality of the modes of production is understood as a determining instance that conditions those elements of a social formation which have traditionally been called the superstructure. If it is assumed—and in fact this is what I will maintain—that subjects are constituted in ideology, an understanding of the determination of this ideological superstructure by the economic base is crucial for an investigation of the subject's determination/formation/constitution by material instances.

If, for example, there is a break between two successive modes of production, such that the later one contains within itself none or only very few of the elements of the preceding one, then it will be hard to account for 'superstructural' phenomena that have persisted over centuries and millennia or for ones that retrospectively appear to be 'ahead of their time.' Also, if the modes of production follow a schema of necessity, this mechanistic conception will also affect the superstructure in a way we have yet to determine. So by stating that 'circumstances make men' or 'social being determines consciousness' and defining what material conditions are, we still have not given an account of the mechanism and form of the determination of the subject by material instances. In order to do so it will be necessary to briefly present the metaphor of base and superstructure (or infrastructure and superstructure) and introduce the concept of ideology.

A Vulgar Interjection: Base and Superstructure

The metaphor of *base and superstructure* is most explicitly formulated by Marx in the famous introduction to his *Contribution to a Critique of Political Economy* where he writes:

> In the social production of their existence, men inevitably enter into definite relations, which are independent of their will, namely relations of production appropriate to a given stage in the development of their material forces of production. The totality of these relations of production constitutes the economic structure of society, the real foundation, on which arises a legal and political superstructure and to which correspond definite forms of social consciousness. (Marx 1999, p. 2)

This edificial metaphor *seems* to propose a base on top of which a superstructure is built, the latter being an effect of the former or in some other way corresponding to it. The vulgar Marxist theory of the levels of base and superstructure posits just that: The superstructural phenomena correspond to or express the economic, which is the primary determinant of social reality. Everything that happens on the level of the material base will have an effect on the (immaterial) superstructure. Characterizations of Marxian theory as 'economistic,' 'monistic,' 'simplistic,' or 'mechanistic' determinism' (Mantz 2008, p. 19) stem from such an interpretation and are still (or especially) virulent today.

For certain kinds of Soviet Marxism, for instance—particularly the excrescence of Stalinism—the supposed causal relationship between 'economy' and the rest of society was the basis for its insistence on the primacy of productive forces. The 'productionist ideology,' which saw the superstructure of culture, ideology, law, and the state as a mere expression of the 'base,' invoked the Marxian metaphor to justify the notion that 'the infrastructural change in forces of production...' will be enough to 'more or less rapidly transform the whole superstructure'(Jameson 2002, p. 22), including the ideological sphere and forms of subjectivity.

Similar explanations of 'superstructural' phenomena can also be found in literary criticism that analyzes cultural productions as epiphenomena or expressions of material social structures (by only explaining the text in terms of 'class interest' or as a mere reflection of the respective material conditions). Another example are sociologies of knowledge that approach 'cultural structures of knowledge' as an ideational reality that has its real *foundation* in 'social structures that are themselves not ideational but material' (Reckwitz 2002, p. 198).

The classical model presented here is reproduced in Fig. 3.2.[11]

As depicted, there are two spheres separated by a line, one of which (superstructure) rests on the other (base). Unsurprisingly, such a model is too simplistic and distorts what Marx (and Engels) had in mind. As Jakubowski shows in *Ideology and Superstructure in Historical Materialism*, it 'is a complete mistake to think that Marx' differentiation between base and superstructure was an absolute distinction between two different, unoverlapping spheres' (Jakubowski 1990, p. 37). And it would be an equally big mistake to assume that what is called 'the base' unilaterally determines the 'superstructural' level. Furthermore, juxtaposing the material with the cultural/political/legal/ideological is misleading because it fails to recognize the material character of non-economic reality. This juxtaposition (material and its other) has the potential to be mistaken for the differentiation of social being and consciousness. Neither can the superstructure be identified as consciousness, nor is consciousness

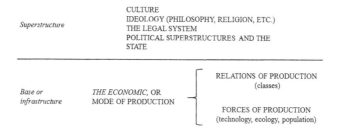

Fig. 3.2   Base and superstructure

an exclusively immaterial abstraction, but is, as conscious being (*Bewusst-sein*), an aspect of material life (cf. ibid., p. 23). We will get back to this in a moment. For now it will suffice to briefly suggest a less mechanistic interpretation of the concept of base and superstructure.

Apart from the section quoted above, Marx makes use of the term in his *The Eighteenth Brumaire of Louis Bonaparte*, where he writes: 'On the different forms of property, the social conditions of existence, arises an entire superstructure of different and peculiarly formed sentiments, delusions, modes of thought and outlooks on life' (Marx 2002, p. 43). Here, it denotes something that cannot be readily identified with the political and legal superstructure. Rather, it is 'the whole "ideology" of the class: its "form of consciousness"; its constitutive ways of seeing itself in the world' (Williams 1977, p. 76). It already becomes clear that 'superstructure' refers not to a fixed and definite aspect of social reality, but to a 'very broad and indeterminate concept' (Jakubowski 1990, p. 37) that encompasses a multitude of things and processes—ideology being one of them.

A letter Engels wrote to Bloch in 1890 can help to further clarify the status of the superstructural. In it he declares that according to the materialist conception of history 'the production and reproduction of real life constitutes *in the last instance* the determining factor of history.' And he adds: 'Neither Marx nor I ever maintained more. Now when someone comes along and distorts this to mean that the economic factor is the *sole* determining factor, he is converting the former proposition into a meaningless, abstract and absurd phrase.' All the various elements of the superstructure exercise an influence on the course of history and the social and 'in many cases determine for the most part their *form*' (Engels 1934, pp. 82–83). The economic base is one aspect that determines a social reality. However, it is a privileged one, because in the last instance it is the determining component.

It should not be forgotten that it is both a spatial and architectural metaphor that we are concerned with. There is no such thing as a base or a superstructure out there. A reification, which denies this, turns it into a dead metaphor that loses its power to draw attention to aspects of reality that cannot otherwise be singled out and presented as discernible entities. Simply because of the interrelatedness of all elements that constitute something like a social 'whole,' there can be no clear separation of two distinct levels. Still, what can be extracted from this conceptual distinction and the image of a base on which a structure is built is that without this groundwork the upper floors are unable to stand. That is to say: without the production of material life (without the production of the means to survive), there would be no political, legal, ideological etc. superstructure. The other feature the metaphor makes visible is that the base exerts some kind of effectivity on the superstructure. However, it is not a direct determination, and there are multiple factors that affect both what happens in the narrowly defined economic as well as 'non-economic' sphere. In conclusion, we can say that there is no economic determinism implied in the metaphor; that base and superstructure can neither be equated with material vs. immaterial nor with being vs. consciousness; and that the mechanism of effectivity at work remains opaque at this point. We will return to this problem shortly. First, however, Marx's notions of ideology will be presented to understand more clearly how the subject is determined or conditioned by material conditions.

MATERIAL CONDITIONS AND THE SUBJECT: THREE NOTIONS OF IDEOLOGY IN MARX

Ideology is one of the central concepts in contemporary Marxism. It is also one of the most loosely defined terms, not only in Marxism but also in social and cultural theory in general.[12] What Jameson wrote more than 40 years ago, namely that 'for the most part Marxism itself has conceived of ideology only in the crudest fashion as a type of mystification or deliberate class distortion, and has failed to provide a really systematic exploration of superstructures' (Jameson 1974, p. 102) still holds true, albeit to a lesser degree.[13] The claim that will be made in this section is that three different but related notions of ideology can be identified in Marx's writings. All of them imply a more or less specific relation of the subject to its material conditions. They must, however, be modified and revised in order to arrive at a conception of ideology that can account for the constitution of the subject and simultaneously explicate the relation to its material determinants or conditions. What complicates this task is that Marx himself was never really concerned with developing a theory of ideology (or the subject, for that matter), let alone giving a concise definition. Accordingly, we will have to extract the implicit hints to his notions of ideology.

In *The German Ideology*, it will be suggested, we find ideology conceived as *illusion* or (*necessarily*) *false consciousness*. In the *The Eighteenth Brumaire of Louis Bonaparte* it appears as a *limitation* to the thinking of subjects. Finally, in *Capital*, we encounter a form of ideology that can be identified with *commodity fetishism*.

The German Ideology

The first conception of ideology we will examine here describes it as a distorted view of reality that is derivative of the real, objective processes, the material production and the material intercourse of individuals. Ideology is here conceived of as a set of ideas or a form of consciousness. The emergence of ideology thus defined is closely tied to developments in the division of labor. Only with the separation of mental and material labor can ideology proper (including morality, religion, metaphysics etc.) appear. Prior to this, consciousness is exclusively consciousness of the immediate surroundings, practices, interactions, and so forth. In other words, there is no separation of *life* and *consciousness.*

> Division of labor only becomes truly such from the moment when a division of material and mental labor appears. (The first form of ideologists, priests, is concurrent.) From this moment onwards consciousness can really flatter itself that it is something other than consciousness of existing practice, that it really represents something without representing something real; from now on consciousness is in a position to emancipate itself from the world and to proceed to the formation of 'pure' theory, theology, philosophy, ethics, etc. (Marx and Engels 1965, p. 43)

So here, it seems, ideology corresponds roughly with consciousness that has become detached from immediate practice and furthermore can loosely be identified with religion and philosophy (which is also due to the target of the text's polemic). The material and real division of labor that really separates mental from material labor constitutes a part of social reality. So, in a sense, there is an independence of thought from practical activity. The ideologies of 'pure theory' and the forms of consciousness they presuppose might have a 'semblance of independence'—which can, however, not be retained in face of the fact that 'men, developing their material production and their material intercourse, alter, along with this their real existence, their thinking and the products of their thinking' (Marx and Engels 1965, p. 38).[14] If human beings alter their thinking in material processes, and we stop there, it would appear that all consciousness is merely ideological as soon as it is conscious of something that is not immediately present. It also implies that the subject is not autonomous in their thinking but that ideas and the way the subject thinks about themself and their relationship with other subjects within a social reality is either consciousness of practice or abstract consciousness that might flatter itself to be autonomous but in fact is not. The argumentative target of this assertion is evidently a philosophy that asserts not only the autonomy, but also the primacy of ideas. The German philosophy that asserts this primacy also claims that to change the world one merely has to change the 'ideas'—this is the specifically German ideology. Inverting this idealism, it now looks like the assertion is simply countered with its opposite: ideas are not autonomous but derivative and not primary but secondary.

For Marx and Engels, ideology first and foremost denotes a distorted, obscured, 'false' consciousness that expresses something real. Consciousness is conscious existence (*Bewusstsein*) and the subjects' existence is their actual, material life-process. Let us say that thought that believes itself to be independent of material factors is not ideology per se, but permits the existence of false consciousness. If then in 'all ideology men and their circumstances appear upside-down as in a camera obscura, this phenomenon arises just as much from their historical life-process as the inversion of objects on the retina does from their physical life-process.' All ideology is false consciousness and a conscious expression (an imaginary one) of their 'real relationships and activities, of their production and intercourse and of their social and political organization' (ibid., p. 37). Subjects' ideas falsely express their real relationship to material conditions. Without expounding this point, it should be remarked that the notion of (necessarily) false consciousness is tied to the—later partially withdrawn—idea of alienation which describes the process by which the division of labor leads to conditions in which the collective practical activity of the production of material life and the relations of production in this process are experienced by the subjects as something alien to them. They appear as supra-human, natural relations the individuals do not control but are controlled by.

The material conditions in capitalist societies are marked by the prevalent class antagonism between bourgeoisie and proletariat. The exploited and oppressed class of individuals bereft of means of production and forced to sell their labor power stands opposed to the class of owners of the means of production that extracts surplus-value from the workers. These relations of production are also relations of dominance. The dominant class has at its disposal the means of material production and thereby constitutes the ruling material force. It also controls and has access to the means of mental production (such as time and other material resources), which makes it the ruling intellectual force. Whence, 'the ideas of the ruling class are in every epoch the ruling ideas' and 'the ruling ideas are nothing more than the ideal expression of the dominant material relationships, the dominant material relationships grasped as ideas' (Marx and Engels 1965, p. 60). The ideas of those who lack the means of mental production are thus largely subject to those ruling ideas. There exists, then, a dominant ideology that expresses the dominant material relationships. But it expresses them in a certain way that does not 'represent' or 'reflect' but distorts them by essentializing, naturalizing, biologizing, and universalizing the dominant material conditions. Ideology stabilizes relations of exploitation by presenting these relations as natural, rational, and universal. The dominant ideas take the form of universality and represent themselves as expressing the common interest of all members of the social formation. Hence, ideology now understood as dominant ideology comprises abstractions that justify 'the way things work.'

Although ideology serves the function of rationalizing and validating a particular form of production and property relations, it should not be misunderstood as propaganda or deliberate misinformation by greedy capitalists who are anxious to secure their wealth. It is precisely the point Marx is trying to make that ideological distortions do not have their origin in the minds of individuals, but that one should explain 'the formation of ideas from material practice.' Following this, 'false consciousness' does not disappear when it is met with better arguments for a 'right consciousness'—at least in most cases. It is the practical overthrow of the actual social relations which gave rise to this 'idealistic humbug' that is needed to abolish the falsified abstractions.

What becomes evident in this description of ideology is that Marx and Engels suppose a problematic dichotomy of 'real' processes, relations, practices, conditions, human beings, etc. (the material reality) on the one hand and mere 'ideas' on the other. The use of words like 'reflexes,' 'echoes' and 'sublimates' in the characterization of ideas and their being bound to material reality seems at once to relegate those ideas and perform a division of something presented as indissociable in the rest of the text: consciousness and action (cf. e.g. Eagleton 1991, p. 75). In this, to use Althusser's accusation, 'positivist-mechanistic' and thus 'not-yet-Marxist conception of ideology' (Althusser, p. 173), meaning is dislocated from practice. It is something secondary; an effect of what is real and material. As Raymond Williams remarks, the polemic in *The German Ideology* repeats the idealist dualism of 'ideas' and 'material reality,' but with its priorities reversed. 'The emphasis on consciousness as inseparable from conscious existence, and then on conscious existence as inseparable from material social processes, is in effect lost in the use of this deliberately degrading vocabulary' (Williams 1977, p. 59).[15] Meaning and practice as well as consciousness and material social processes cannot be conceptualized as simply opposing each other. Their inseparability is a theme that runs through many of Marx's other writings and will be an important aspect with regards to the constitution of the subject in material conditions.

The Eighteenth Brumaire of Louis Bonaparte

The second variant of ideology that I wish to propose can be found in Marx's *The Eighteenth Brumaire of Louis Bonaparte* and can be described as *structural limitation* or what Fredric Jameson calls 'ideological closure' (Jameson 2002, p. 37). In his analysis of the political events surrounding Louis-Napoleon Bonaparte's *coup d'état* in 1851, Marx does not expose the 'false consciousness' of the ruling class's ideologues, but grants 'a considerable degree of autonomy and independent effect... to ideas, ideologies and other such elements of the "superstructure"' (Cowling and Martin 2002, p. 6). That is also to say, he grants the subjects he identifies as political actors a degree of autonomy that goes beyond any direct determination by their social and material situation. The 'ideas' subjects have about their position in the social totality of nineteenth-century France are not portrayed as effluence of their 'real' positions, but enter a complex interplay with the material factors. Their ideas, i.e. the way they position themselves and others in a symbolic structure, materially affects the political situation. One of the central quotes from this text reads: 'Men make their own history, but they do not make it just as they please in circumstances they choose for themselves; rather they make it in present circumstances, given and inherited' (Marx 2002, p. 19).[16] The given and inherited circumstances can 'be considered as *materiality*' (Jameson 2004, p. xxiii). In this materiality that is the concrete historical situation, subjects act and also think about the way they act. In their thinking, Marx proposes, they are limited by boundaries imposed by the economic itself. This is not the same as false consciousness that inverts and distorts the material world with illusions.

Bourgeois thinking that attempts to comprehend and explicate the whole social world it inhabits can produce coherent systems of thought that reconcile the subject with social reality—but it is bound to hit the wall at some point. For instance, there is misery in the world and wealth is distributed incredibly unevenly. This situation is made comprehensible within limits that are *not* beyond the limits of capitalism.[17] A coherent explanation of the world is necessarily sought in other forms to intelligibly represent it. In *History and Class Consciousness*, Lukács argues for a similar view on ideology when he writes that it 'is the objective result of the economic set-up, and is neither arbitrary, subjective nor psychological' and that bourgeois thought 'becomes obscured as soon as it is called upon to face problems that remain within its jurisdiction but which point beyond the limits of capitalism' (Lukács 1972, p. 54). Such a view explodes the confines that ideology understood as 'reflection' or 'echoing' was subjected to. It expands the scope and the leeway of ideological practice while acknowledging the limits of thinking set by the economic reality.

Žižek evokes *strategies of containment* or *limitations* that have a semblance to what Marx had in mind when he keeps illustrating the strangeness of our current predicament by showing that it is apparently easier for us to imagine the end of all life on earth than to think of the possibility of the end of capitalism, i.e. the comparatively modest task of grasping the possibility of different ways to organize the production and distribution of our means of subsistence.[18] Alien invasions, natural catastrophes, divine intervention—all are thinkable by the ideological subject; but only as contained in this mode of production. We think within a *symbolic order* that cannot be detached from economic conditions.

To give an example—borrowed from Jameson—that elucidates what is meant here, we can call Hegel's notion of Absolute Spirit a limited thinking or a *strategy of containment*, 'which allows what can be thought to seem internally coherent in its own terms, while repressing the unthinkable (in this case, the very possibility of collective praxis) which lies beyond its boundaries' (Jameson 2002, p. 38). Hegel was limited in his thinking not because he lacked the intellectual capacity to understand what the real driving force behind history was. Nor was his great philosophical system bourgeois propaganda that veiled the absurdity of the misery in the world with abstract concepts that provided coherence and comprehensibility. It was limits imposed by social reality itself that prevented him from—polemically speaking—becoming Marx. Ideology is not directly correlating to class affiliation or origin, either. The limitation is not restricted to a particular (ruling) class. In the *Brumaire*, Marx writes:

> What makes them [the intellectuals that neither are themselves 'shopkeepers' nor necessarily share the economic conditions of the petty bourgeoisie, JB] representatives of the petty bourgeoisie is the fact that in their heads

they do not transcend the limitations that others have not surmounted in life, that they are therefore driven to the same problems and solutions in theory that material interests and social life pose for others in practice. In general terms this is the relationship between the *political and literary representatives* of a class to the class that they represent. (Marx 1988, p. 45)

In short, the material reality that the subject is involved in *limits* the subject's autonomy not only with regards to the individual's socio-economic situation that puts them in relations of production that they did not chose, but also limits the subject in the way they think about and symbolically positions themself in that material reality.

Capital

There exists a third theory of ideology, implicit in Marx's *Capital*—that is, the fetishism of the commodity, or simply *commodity fetishism*. It is largely identical with what Lukács later called *commodity reification* and with what contemporary Marxism terms *reification* in general. What Marx shows in a chapter of *Capital* titled 'The Fetishism of the Commodity and Its Secret' is that in commodity-producing societies (which is the same as to say capitalist societies) the relations between subjects take the form of relations between things, and the relations between the products of their labor (commodities) appear as social relations.

A thing that is produced by human labor and satisfies needs—as use-value—is not mysterious. But as soon as it takes the form of a commodity with exchange-value 'it is a very strange thing, abounding in metaphysical subtleties and theological niceties' (Marx 1990, 1976, p. 163). The secret of the commodity lies

> simply in the fact that the commodity reflects the social characteristics of men's own labor as objective characteristics of the products of labor themselves, as the socio-natural properties of these things. Hence it also reflects the social relation of the producers to a sum total of labor as a social relation between objects, a relation which exists apart from and outside the producers. Through this substitution, the products of labor become commodities, sensuous things which are at the same time supra-sensible or social. (Marx 1990, pp. 164–165)

Capitalism is the only mode of production in which things are produced *primarily for exchange*. Only in a commodity-producing society do individuals relate everything to *exchange-value*. That commodities *have* exchange-value, even what that exchange-value is, presents itself as a natural *property* of things (like weight, or color). Their value, however, has absolutely no connection to their physical properties, but 'the measure of the expenditure of human labor-power by its duration takes on the form of the magnitude of the value of the products of labor' (Marx 1990, p. 164). It would seem that this is another ideological inversion, whereby the relations between things *appear* as social relations and that the explication of this unfortunate fantasy would be the end of it. But if this *fetishism*, which mystifies objects by ascribing them an inherent exchange-value, is an illusion it is an *objective illusion*. Or in Althusser's words: 'this appearance is not subjective at all, but, on the contrary, objective through and through, the "illusion" of the "consciousness" and perceptions being itself secondary, and dislocated by the structure of this primary, purely objective 'illusion'!' (Althusser and Balibar 1997, p. 191). The subjects *cannot but see it this way*; commodity fetishism has a *material objectivity*.

In capitalism, producers (of services or other commodities) enter social relations with one another. However, they come into social contact with each other only in the moment they exchange their products of labor. So, 'the labor of the private individual manifests itself as an element of the total labor of society only through the relations which the act of exchange establishes between the products, and, through their mediation, between the producers' (Marx 1990, p. 165). To the producers, the social relations of their private labors appear as what they really are: material (*dingliche*) relations between persons and social relations between things. It should be added—without going into detail—that money, as the universal equivalent, adds another dimension to the fetishism. While commodities seem to naturally *have* exchange-value, money apparently *is* exchange-value. It is the incarnation of an abstraction. The absurd form of money that relates all commodities to itself as the universal incarnation of abstract human labor 'conceals the social character of private labor and the social relations between the individual workers, by making those relations appear as relations between material objects, instead of revealing them plainly' (Marx 1990, pp. 168–169).

In the exchange producers equate their different kinds of labor as human labor, precisely by the operation of exchange that equates different products of labor to each other as values. They are doing it, but they are not aware of it, Marx says. But even if they knew what they were doing, they would still do it. The forms of thought that spring from commodity fetishism 'are socially valid, and therefore objective, for the relations of production belonging to this historically determined mode of social production, i.e. commodity production' (Marx 1990, p. 169). What makes this fetishism an *ideology* is not that it is *false*, but that the objective laws of commodity exchange are taken to be universal 'socio-natural' facts which are independent of a historically determined mode of social production.

What does this objective illusion of commodity fetishism imply for a conception of the subject? We can look at Lukács's theory of *reification* to get a better idea of these implications. Lukács argues that in the process of the *commodification* of society it is not only the *relations* of subjects that appear as relations of things, but the subjects themselves encounter each other as *reified* things. Relating to other individuals as 'things' becomes 'second nature'—'men's consciousness' is subjugated to 'the forms in which this reification finds expression.' At the same time, 'the commodity can only be understood in its undistorted essence when it becomes the universal category of society as a whole' (Lukács 1972, p. 86).

In Marx's time, and arguably in Lukács's time as well, commodification had not yet reached its pinnacle. With the progressing commodification of culture, which Adorno and Horkheimer describe in the chapter on *Culture Industry: Enlightenment as Mass Deception* in their *Dialectic of Enlightenment* (Adorno and Horkheimer 1997, pp. 120–166) commodification and objectivation had already reached the sphere of aesthetic production that before had appeared to lie outside the range of the logic of exchange-value. Jameson's analysis in *Postmodernism. Or, the Cultural Logic of Late Capitalism* agrees with Adorno and Horkheimer, insofar as he asserts that culture 'has become a product in its own right' (Jameson 1991, p. x). But going further, he argues that in the postmodern period the commodity form has colonized nearly all of social reality. This process unfolds via a

> prodigious expansion of capital into hitherto uncommodified areas. This purer capitalism of our own time thus eliminates the enclaves of precapitalist organization it had hitherto tolerated and exploited in a tributary way. One is tempted to speak, in this connection of a new and historically original penetration and colonization of Nature and the Unconscious. (Jameson 1991, p. 36)

In a world where commodification becomes total, it stretches not 'merely' into nature and the unconscious, but commodifies human subjects as well (cf. Jameson 1991, p. 11). This colonization reaches well into our most intimate personal, romantic, and sexual relations in which subjects now *universally* enter abstract, rational relations 'for which exchange is the model' (Adorno 1999, p. 248). Étienne Balibar gives a different perspective, which is, nevertheless, compatible with the other ones:

> if the constitution of objectivity in fetishism does not depend on the prior givenness of a subject, a consciousness or a reason, it does, by contrast, constitute subjects which are a part of objectivity itself or which are, in other words, given in experience *alongside 'things,'* alongside commodities, *and in a relation to them.* These subjects are not constituent, but constituted; they are quite simply 'economic subjects' or, more exactly, they are all individuals who, in bourgeois society, are first of all economic subjects. (Balibar 2007, p. 67)

Ideology in the form of commodity fetishism is qualified by four stark differences to both of the other conceptualizations. (1) Commodity fetishism is specific to capitalism. Only in commodity-producing and commodity-exchanging social formations can such an ideology and the forms of subjectivity emerging from it arise. (2) Ideology, thus understood, exists in *practices* and not just in the consciousness of subjects. The exchange of commodities for money and the enactment of the principle of exchange in social relations is something *we do*. In the exchange the relations are material (*dingliche*) relations between persons and social relations between things, so that: (3) The inversion that takes place is not one in the subjects' minds (a misrecognition of the origins of exchange-value in social labor) but is inherent in social reality itself. In the curious inversion between subjects and their material conditions of existence it doesn't just appear as if commodities exercise a material power over social relations: they actually do. Economic subjects depend on selling *commodities* (labor power included) as much as buying them (just to satisfy their needs) and can therefore not step out of fetishism.[19] (4) Ideology in economic practice blurs the boundary between what we encountered as *base and superstructure*. This mode of ideology does not reflect an inverted image of material reality, but an image of inverted reality. It does not do so in the 'ideas' of the subjects, but in their economic *practices* that would seemingly belong to the economic base. We will revisit the concept of base and superstructure as well as that of the mode of production in a moment.

It should be noted that the three types of ideology proposed, different as they may be, are not mutually exclusive. They highlight different ways in which subjects think, represent, and live their relation to their material conditions of existence. It is clear that they contradict each other in certain aspects. For instance, in *The German Ideology* the consciousness about the primacy of ideas could be exposed as false, as an *illusion*, while commodity fetishism resists such intellectual enlightenment. Orthodox Marxist dreams of the proletariat as the *subject of history* that can break free of the illusions of false consciousness seem misplaced in the face of the ideology of commodity reification, which surely has its grip on the honest worker in the factory as well.

We have now established the key aspects of Marx's theory in regards to the material conditions and the ideological subject. The material conditions have been loosely identified with the mode of production, and their materiality could be shown to consist not only of tangible matter but also and especially of relations, practices, and processes. The mode of production specific to a social formation produces subjects and subjectivities appropriate to that particular formation. The subject's intellectual capacity is not constitutive of all reality but constituted in a social reality that is the result of practical human activity. Ideology was then introduced as that which relates the subject to its material conditions and constitutes it. The three different kinds of ideology refined the forms in which material conditions condition the (thinking and acting) subject. What has not yet been established, however, is *how* the human subject is constructed or constituted. So far we lack the precise *mechanism* by which material reality brings the subject into existence and in (subjectively meaningful) relation to this reality. We don't yet know how subjects are *produced*. This is mainly due to the fact that Marx (and several generations of Marxists after him) 'failed to provide a really systematic exploration of superstructures' (Jameson 1974, p. 102). As of now, the subject appears as a category that is under the sway of material conditions that, albeit produced and reproduced *by* real individuals, face it as an alien force outside of it. The autonomy of the subject that was so central to German idealism might figure as a potential to be realized, but lost its status as the foundation of philosophy.[20] Even though it should be clear by now that Marx does not argue for a *mechanistic determinism,* the realm of subjective freedom (or '*agency*,' to use a more fashionable term) that stands opposed to that of necessity is not thoroughly explored. Instead of holding this against him—he has written and done more than enough for Marxism—we should turn to some of his disciples. More precisely, it is Althusser's and Jameson's Marxisms that will be introduced as a helpful refinement and extension of Marxian thought with regard to materiality, ideology, and the subject. In a first step the concept of the *mode of production* (and with it the metaphor of base and superstructure) is briefly revisited. In a second step Althusser's *Ideological State Apparatuses* are presented and the definition of ideology is specified as *a representation of the imaginary relationship of individuals to their real conditions of existence.*

NOTES

1. Which does not mean that materialism is merely a derivative theory. As Coward and Ellis remark, 'materialism... is not the simple opposite of idealism: it is the repressed of Western philosophy, in that it has never been dominant and that materialism can be found in contradictory moments of idealist philosophy' (Coward and Ellis 1977, p. 83).
2. For elaborations on this point, see e.g. the introductory texts by Étienne Balibar (2007, pp. 13ff) and Peter Singer (2000, pp. 41ff).
3. Idealists, such as Hegel and Fichte, might have emphasized that our activities (our interactions with the object-world) change the way we perceive reality, but idealism 'does not know real, sensuous activity as such' (Marx 2010, p. 3).
4. Marx never used this term. It was coined later by Engels.
5. To understand the materialist dialectic or the materialist conception of history as a simple inversions of Hegelian thought is, however, problematic, as we will see when we are concerned with the question of how material conditions determine consciousness and subjectivity (for a lengthier account of this problem, see e.g. Althusser 1969, pp. 88–128).
6. Production can be defined as 'the transformation of specific raw materials into specific products by labour using specific tools. It is productive activity that marks human society, and the form of the production of the material means of subsistence that finally determines the form of a particular society' (Coward and Ellis 1977, p. 63).
7. Material forces and not ideas. While in Hegel the same dialectical movement of contradiction and resolution drives history, it all happens in the ideal realm. And Hegel's young antecedents, eager to change the world, thought that changed ideas—different views on the world—could revolutionize society.
8. For an exposition of the different modes of production also see Marx et al. (1965, c1964).
9. There is a 'causal primacy to the **mode of production** over ideas/the **ideological** sphere in social life' (Walker and Gray 2007, p. 214).

10. The opening of *The Communist Manifesto* can be used to illustrate this: 'The history of all hitherto existing society is the history of class struggles. Freeman and slave, patrician and plebeian, lord and serf, guild-master and journeyman, in a word, oppressor and oppressed, stood in constant opposition to one another, carried on an uninterrupted, now hidden, now open fight, a fight that each time ended, either in a revolutionary reconstitution of society at large, or in the common ruin of the contending classes' (Marx and Engels 1998, p. 3). The class struggle ended either in revolution and a change in the mode of production or in the common ruin of the contending classes. No mechanical necessity guarantees the movement from one stage to another.

11. Cf. Jameson (2002, p. 17).

12. Terry Eagleton identifies 16 'definitions of ideology currently in circulation: (a) the process of production of meanings, signs and values in social life; (b) a body of ideas characteristic of a particular social group or class; (c) ideas which help to legitimate a dominant political power; (d) false ideas which help to legitimate a dominant political power; (e) systematically distorted communication; (f) that which offers a position for a subject; (g) forms of thought motivated by social interests; (h) identity thinking; (i) socially necessary illusion; (j) the conjuncture of discourse and power; (k) the medium in which conscious social actors make sense of their world; (l) action-oriented sets of beliefs; (m) the confusion of linguistic and phenomenal reality; (n) semiotic closure; (o) the indispensable medium in which individuals live out their relations to a social structure; (p) the process whereby social life is converted to a natural reality' (Eagleton 1991, pp. 1–2). We could surely find more.

13. There have been numerous attempts in recent years to refine the concept, some of which we will be dealing with at a later point. See, e.g. Badiou (2013), Ben Rafael (2003), Decker (2004), Rehmann (2013), and the contributions by Theborn, Bourdieu, Jameson, Eagleton, Rorty, and Žižek in Mapping Ideology (Žižek 1994).

14. In other words: 'Men are the producers of their conceptions, ideas, etc.— real, active men, as they are conditioned by a definite development of their productive forces and of the intercourse corresponding to these, up to its furthest forms' (Marx and Engels 1965, p. 37).

15. Which is not to say that something like false consciousness does not exist. For instance, claiming that global economic inequality is rooted in the biological inferiority of Africans and Asians or explaining it by saying that poor people are poor because they are lazy is certainly false. Just like thinking that the true problem is to be found in 'classism' and would disappear if we all stopped discriminating against the 'less advantaged'.

16. Sartre's whole *Critique of Dialectical Reason* (Sartre 2004) can be described as a commentary on this famous quote (cf. ibid., p. xxiii). Lukacs' theory

of ideology presented in *History and Class Consciousness* (Lukács 1972) was heavily influenced by the whole text as well.

17. In *The Prison-House of Language*, Jameson writes: 'Internally, the structural limitation is nothing more than the total number of permutations and combinations inherently possible in the model in question; while the external limits are set by history itself, which pre-selects a certain number of structural possibilities for actualization, while proscribing others as inconceivable in the social and cultural climate of a given area' (Jameson 1974, pp. 127–128).

18. See, for example *Living in End Times* (Žižek 2011).

19. Terry Eagleton illustrates this nicely: 'The capitalist who has devoured all three volumes of *Capital* knows exactly what he is doing; but he continues to behave as though he did not, because his activity is caught up in the 'objective' fantasy of commodity fetishism' (Eagleton 1991, p. 40).

20. In *The Communist Manifesto*, Marx and Engels write: 'In place of the old bourgeois society, with its classes and class antagonisms, we shall have an association, in which the free development of each is the condition for the free development of all' (Marx and Engels 1998, p. 26).

REFERENCES

Adorno, T. W. (1999). *Critical models.* New York: Columbia University Press.

Adorno, T. W., & Horkheimer, M. (1997). *Dialectic of enlightenment.* London: Verso.

Althusser, L. (1969). *For Marx.* New York: Pantheon Books.

Althusser, L., & Balibar, E. (1997). *Reading Capital.* London: Verso.

Badiou, A. (2013). *Theory of the subject.* London: Bloomsbury Academic.

Balibar, E. (2007). *The philosophy of Marx.* London: Verso.

Ben Rafael, E. (2003). *Sociology and ideology.* Leiden: Brill.

Coward, R., & Ellis, J. (1977). *Language and materialism: Developments in semiology and the theory of the subject.* London, Boston: Routledge & Paul.

Cowling, M., & Martin, J. (2002). Introduction. In K. Marx, M. Cowling, & J. Martin (Eds.), *Marx's eighteenth Brumaire: (Post)modern interpretations* (pp. 1–15). London: Pluto Press.

Decker, J. M. (2004). *Ideology.* Houndmills, Basingstoke: Palgrave Macmillan.

Eagleton, T. (1991). *Ideology: An introduction.* London: Verso.

Engels, F. (1934). Engels to J. Bloch in Berlin. London, September 21, 1890. *New International, 1*(3), 81–85.

Jakubowski, F. (1990). *Ideology and superstructure in historical materialism.* London: Pluto.

Jameson, F. (1974). *The prison-house of language: A critical account of structuralism and Russian formalism.* Princeton, NJ: Princeton University Press.

Jameson, F. (1991). *Postmodernism, or, the cultural logic of late capitalism.* London: Verso.

Jameson, F. (2002). *The political unconscious: Narrative as a socially symbolic act.* London: Routledge.

Jameson, F. (2004). Foreword. In J.-P. Sartre (Ed.), *Critique of dialectical reason* (pp. xiii–xxxiii). London: Verso.

Lukács, G. (1972). *History and class consciousness.* Boston: MIT Press.

Mantz, J. (2008). Materialism. In W. A. Darity (Ed.), *International encyclopedia of the social sciences* (pp. 18–21). Detroit: Macmillan Reference.

Marx, K. (1988). *The eighteenth Brumaire of Louis Bonaparte.* New York, NY: International Publishers.

Marx, K. (1990). *Capital: A critique of political economy.* London: Penguin.

Marx, K. (1999). *A contribution to the critique of political economy.* Moscow: Progress Publishers.

Marx, K. (2002). The eighteenth Brumaire of Louis Bonaparte. In M. Cowling & J. Martin (Eds.), *Marx's eighteenth Brumaire: (Post)modern interpretations* (pp. 19–109). London: Pluto Press.

Marx, K. (2010). Theses on Feuerbach. In K. Marx and F. Engels (Eds.), *Karl Marx and Friedrich Engels works, April 1845–April 1847* (Vol. 5, pp. 3–5). London: Lawrence & Wishart.

Marx, K., & Engels, F. (1965). *The German ideology.* London: Lawrence & Wishart.

Marx, K., & Engels, F. (2010). *Karl Marx and Frederick Engels works, April 1845–April 1847* (Vol. 5). London: Lawrence & Wishart.

Marx, K., Cohen, J., & Hobsbawm, E. J. (1965, c1964). Pre-capitalist economic formations. New York: International Publishers.

Reckwitz, A. (2002). The status of the "material" in theories of culture: From "social structure" to "artefacts". *Theory of Social Behaviour, 32*(2), 195–217.

Rehmann, J. (2013). *Theories of ideology: The powers of alienation and subjection.* Brill: Boston.

Sartre, J.-P. (2004). *Critique of dialectical reason.* London: Verso.

Singer, P. (2000). *Marx: A very short introduction.* Oxford: Oxford University Press.

Walker, D. M., & Gray, D. (2007). *Historical dictionary of Marxism.* Lanham, MD: Scarecrow Press.

Williams, R. (1977). *Marxism and literature.* Oxford: Oxford University Press.

Žižek, S. (Ed.). (1994). *Mapping ideology.* London: Verso.

Žižek, S. (2011). *Living in the end times.* London: Verso.

CHAPTER 4

Structural Causality and Material Ideology

Abstract Althusser's and Jameson's Marxisms are a necessary and helpful refinement of Marxian thought with regard to the concepts of materiality, ideology, and the subject. This chapter retraces the revisions Althusser and Jameson make to Marx's concept of 'modes of production' and shows how these revisions help better understand how material conditions determine or affect the subject and what type of causality exists between the latter. The second part of the chapter deals with Althusser's theory of ideology. Highlighting the important role of practice and insisting on a materialism that does not rely solely on matter or matter in motion in its definition of what is material, it closes with the delineation of the different kinds of materiality implicit in Marxist materialism.

Keywords Louis Althusser • Fredric Jameson • Ideological State Apparatuses • Materialism • Subject • Materiality

Modes of Production and the Ultimately Determining Instance of the Material

Three important revisions to classical Marxist theory, all of which touch upon the idea of *modes of production*, will be suggested in the following pages: (1) The 'base,' or, better,: the mode of production, is not *expressed*

49

J. Beetz, *Materiality and Subject in Marxism, (Post-)Structuralism, and Material Semiotics*, DOI 10.1057/978-1-137-59837-0_4

or *reflected* in ideology, culture, law, the political (what was earlier called 'the superstructure'), but a *structural causality* exists between the whole of the mode of production and its various elements. (2) The characterization of modes of production should not be confined to the narrowly defined economic. The combination of forces of production and relations of production is not identical with the mode of production, but is one—albeit *privileged*—level of this mode. The levels of a mode of production are *semi-autonomous*. (3) In a given social formation there coexist several modes of production, *one of them* being dominant. This can help explain the endurance of social phenomena that stretch over several dominant modes of production, and further weakens economistic and deterministic approaches to Marxian thought. These three points reconfigure what 'material conditions' denotes. And, more importantly, they help us better understand how those conditions determine or affect the subject. Naturally, these amendments can be sketched out only in very broad strokes.

Material conditions have an effect on ideology, culture, politics, and other elements of the social, which have been called 'superstructural' to set them off from the purely economic. But what kind of *effectivity* or *causality* is at work, when it is said that capitalism determines its subjects, or the mode of production conditions culture and politics? How does the economic determine the rest of social reality? Are the material conditions *outside* of the entities and relations they determine? Or is everything in a social formation just an *expression* of a *principle* (that of the commodity or of class antagonisms)? It is here that we can introduce the type of causality that Althusser deems most suited for Marxist theory: *structural causality*. For him, the idea of analyzing the '*presence* of the structure in its *effects*' (Althusser and Balibar 1997, p. 188) is something inherent in Marx's writing, particularly in *Capital*, and not something that has to be added to it or corrected (the title of the chapter, in which he writes about this form of effectivity, is called *Marx's Immense Theoretical Revolution*). But, according to Althusser, the effectivity by which material conditions determine elements of a social formation has been misconstrued to resemble either a mechanical or an expressive effectivity. He claims that:

> 'classical philosophy (the existing Theoretical) had two and only two systems of concepts with which to think effectivity. The mechanistic system, Cartesian in origin, which reduced causality to a *transitive* and analytical effectivity: it could not be made to think the effectivity of a whole on its

elements' and another system 'conceived precisely in order to deal with the effectivity of a whole on its elements: the Leibnizian concept of *expression*. This is the model that dominates Hegel's thought. But it presupposes in principle that the whole in question is reducible to an *inner essence*, of which the elements of the whole are then no more than the phenomenal forms of expression, the inner principle of the essence being present at each point in the whole, such that at each moment it is possible to write the immediately adequate equation: *such and such an element* (economic, political, legal, literary, religious, etc. in Hegel) = *the inner essence of the whole*'. (Althusser and Balibar 1997, pp. 186–187)

The mechanistic system he alludes to is one where, for example, a change on the economic level has a direct effect on cultural production or the way people think (cause and effect). There might be such mechanical effects of the economic on the cultural, but they are not the norm and not what Marx had in mind. The *expressive causality* is one that was more often ascribed to Marx's thinking. In another book, *For Marx*, Althusser gives us a hint as to why:

For Hegel's 'pure' principle of consciousness (of the epoch's consciousness of itself), for the simple internal principle which he conceived as the principle of the intelligibility of all the determinations of a historical people, we have substituted *another simple principle,* its opposite: material life, the economy—a simple principle which in turn becomes the sole principle of the universal intelligibility of all the determinations of a historical people. (Althusser 1969, p. 108)

He exaggerates, but what he means is clear. Marx *could* be understood and *has been* understood as turning Hegel on his head and at once inverting the direction of determination as well: It is not the idea that determines the material world, but material life (the economy) that determines the idea and everything else, all the while maintaining Hegel's principle of expressive causality. This interpretation simply substitutes absolute Spirit with the economic as the driving force behind history and society without seeing the specificity of Marx's notion of effectivity.

Althusser now opposes his *structural causality* to the other two forms of effectivity. In what he proposes, the structure determines its elements while this causality is one with an *absent cause*. Absent, because it is not outside the elements, expressing itself in them. Nor are the effects outside the structure, they 'are not a pre-existing object, element or space in which the structure arrives to *imprint its mark*' (Althusser and Balibar 1997, p. 188). The structure is not a 'whole' that has an inner principle which is expressed. Rather, 'the structure is immanent in its effects, a cause immanent in its effects in the Spinozist sense of the term, that *the whole existence of the structure consists of its effects*, in short that the structure, which is merely a specific combination of its peculiar elements, is nothing outside its effects' (ibid., p. 189). In these quotes, it is not immediately obvious *what* this structure is. Before it becomes clearer, another specification has to be made: different *regions* of this structure determine different *phenomena* in the structure. For instance, there are 'economic phenomena… *determined by a (regional) structure* of the mode of production (Fig. 4.1), itself determined by *the (global) structure* of the mode of production' (ibid., p. 185). The regional structures can now also be conceptualized as *levels in a structure*. Finally, we arrive at a definition of the structure as the (global) mode of production consisting of different levels that correspond to the elements we qualified earlier as belonging to either 'base' or 'superstructure' (cf. Fig. 3.2).

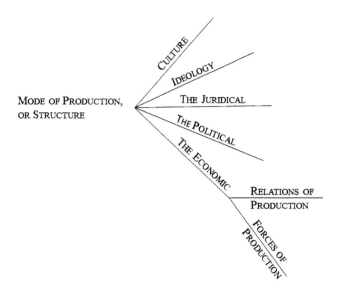

Fig. 4.1 Mode of production (Jameson 2002, p. 21)

The mode of production is no longer identical with the purely economic (consisting of relations of production and forces of production). It is now 'the structure as a whole' or 'the synchronic system of social relations as a whole' (Jameson 2002, p. 21). In the short section on the metaphor of base and superstructure, we saw that the superstructure is conceived to be determined 'in the last instance' by the base and that the edificial metaphor suggests that without its 'fundament' the 'upper floors' could not stand. This still holds true, but the levels of the structure are not univocally determined by the narrowly defined economic; they possess a *semi-autonomy*. Which is to say, while they do not *express* or *reflect* the economic base and are in that sense autonomous (how the state is organized, what culture looks like, what kinds of subject positions are available, etc. is all not an immediate reflection of the economic), they are *semi*-autonomous because they are elements in the structure they constitute. Still, 'in the last instance' they are determined by the economic.

It is, however, never the economic alone that determines a specific phenomenon (there is a multitude of concrete determinations) and so: 'From the first moment to the last, the lonely hour of the "last instance" never comes' (Althusser 1969, p. 113).[1] The relations of production and the forces of production *do not* lose their material force in determining subjects and the non-economic levels, although they do not act alone. This is what Althusser means when he speaks of *overdetermination*. A phenomenon, like the political situation at a given time, the form literary production takes in a historical situation, or the dominant ideology in a specific social formation is never determined by just one factor. There is a multitude of determinants, whose relation is not merely additive, *within the structure* of the mode of production that are not all narrowly economic.

To give an example from Marxist history, we can look at a characterization Lenin gave of twentieth century Russia. In a small text published in *Pravda* (Lenin 1975, pp. 368–369), he writes about *medieval survivals* in capitalist Russia. In short, he says that there are aspects of social reality (like 'landlordism and feudal privileges') in Russia that are not results of the capitalist mode of production, but have survived throughout the centuries, exceeding in their life-span that of the dominant mode of production they emerged in. How are these *survivals* to be explained if (capitalist) economy is the only determining instance for the whole of society? Other examples are easy to find in contemporary late capitalism.

This leads us to the last assertion concerning the concept of the mode of production in Marxism: In each social formation there exist overlapping modes of production, while only one of them is the dominant. This idea is taken from Jameson's Marxist hermeneutics established in *The Political Unconscious* and was initially used to analyze the 'ideology of form' in literary texts. It is, however, relevant in the present context because 'the notion of overlapping modes of production... has indeed the advantage of allowing us to short-circuit the false problem of the priority of the economic' (Jameson 2002, p. 85). It also helps to better account for the mechanism of determination by the material conditions. Jameson, writing about the interpretation of literature, asserts that 'the temptation to classify texts according to the appropriate mode of production is thereby removed, since the texts emerge in a space in which we may expect them to be crisscrossed and intersected by a variety of impulses from contradictory modes of production all at once' (ibid., p. 81). What is true for the production of literature is true for the production of ideologies and subjects as well.

We can make the relatively unproblematic claim that subjects in the western world are *gendered* subjects, i.e. subjects who, as a part of their subjectivity, are for the most part either male or female. We can then make the bolder claim that sexism and patriarchal structures of domination exist, which cannot be explained by some biological essence or disposition. If sexism and the patriarchal are superstructural phenomena that are determined by the economic base, it will be hard to account for the fact that the separation of genders/sexes and the power structures connected to it have persisted (albeit in varying forms) time periods spanning several 'modes of production.' From the perspective of *overlapping modes of production,* in contrast, they

> are to be grasped as the sedimentation and the virulent survival of forms of alienation specific to the oldest mode of production of human history, with its division of labor between men and women, and its division of power between youth and elder. (Ibid., p. 85)

In Jameson's approach, an

> analysis of the ideology of form... should reveal the formal persistence of such archaic structures of alienation... beneath the overlay of all the more recent and historically original types of alienation—such as political domination and commodity reification—which have become dominants of that

most complex of all cultural revolutions, late capitalism, in which all the earlier modes of production in one way or another structurally coexist. (Ibid.)

Proposing an overlap of modes of production is not the same thing as abandoning the concept of those modes altogether. The concept is merely refined and it is suggested that what has been designated a mode of production (e.g. capitalism) never exists in a pure state. There always persist or emerge ways to think and to act that are either reminiscent of older structures or anticipatory of social relations yet to come (they are 'ahead of their time'). Considering the modes as overlapping, also points to the semi-autonomy of levels, in that it underlines the fact that changes in the economic do not immediately trigger appropriate changes on the other levels.

Following these brief elaborations on Althusser's and Jameson's refinements of Marxian theory, we can now turn to the mechanism by which subjects are constituted in relation to the material conditions described above. Here, *ideology* will be examined in the role it plays in the reproduction of relations of production. The concept of ideology we turn to describes the latter as having a *material* reality that derives its materiality from its existence in *practices*. These practices are *representations of the imaginary relationship of individuals to their real conditions of existence*. I will argue that Althusser's theory of ideology, while it is consistent with what we have established so far, introduces (almost in passing) a dimension largely left out till present, which we will be occupied with in Chap. 5 and which is that of the Symbolic, or more specifically, the *materiality of language*.

IDEOLOGY AS THE MATERIAL PRACTICES OF REPRESENTING THE IMAGINARY RELATIONSHIP OF SUBJECTS TO THEIR REAL, MATERIAL CONDITIONS OF EXISTENCE

In every social formation, or *structure*, there exists a dominant mode of production in which the process of production is accomplished through 'productive forces in and under definite relations of production' (Althusser 1972, p. 128). These *conditions* of production must constantly be *reproduced*, otherwise a social formation that produces its means of subsistence 'would not last a year' (ibid.). We have already introduced the distinction between the means of production and labor power, which together comprise the productive forces. It is easy to see that the means of production have to be reproduced. Machines must be repaired or renewed, buildings have to be fixed, and exhausted raw materials need to be replaced etc., just to keep producing.

At the same time, labor power has to be reproduced. This reproduction is not reducible to the 'generational replacement' of labor power in the form of 'biological reproduction' (Vogel *et al.* 2013, p. 146), which has been largely ignored by the (predominantly male) Marxist tradition and which points again to the sexist divisions of labor mentioned above.[2] But it also means that the mental and physical capacity of individuals to produce use-value (in capitalism: commodities) has to be renewed, which is ensured in various ways. First and foremost, labor power is given the material means sufficient to reproduce itself in the form of wages.[3] Keeping the laborers alive at a certain level of contentment is not enough, however. Labor power must also be competent; it has to be '(diversely) skilled and therefore reproduced as such' (ibid., p. 131). Such reproduction is achieved by means of apprenticeships, schools, universities and other instances where 'know-how' is imparted. To these, Althusser adds another requirement in the reproduction of labor power: subjection to the ruling ideology. For him, '*it is in the forms and under the forms of ideological subjection that provision is made for the reproduction of the skills of labor power*' (ibid., p. 133). Although this gives us an idea about the role of ideology in the reproduction of conditions of production, it is still not evident what exactly ideology is—or what subjection is. Althusser approaches this problem from the perspective of the reproduction of *relations of production*. In his seminal text on *Ideology and Ideological State Apparatuses* (Althusser 1972), he attempts to account for the ways this reproduction of relations of production is secured. In our present context only a few important aspects will interest us, so it will be enough to outline the theoretical context this theory of ideology is embedded in.

It has already been shown that in Althusser's writings the static model of base and superstructure has been revised without denying the 'determination in the last instance' by the economic. Furthermore, the relative autonomy of the different levels that were initially described as superstructural and the concept of structural causality were explained. Against this background, Althusser offers a preliminary answer to the question of how the reproduction of relations of production is guaranteed: It is secured by the semi-autonomous (superstructural) levels of the legal-political and the ideological. Both of those levels are tied to *the State* in one way or another.

In orthodox Marxist tradition '[t]he State is a "machine" of repression, which enables the ruling classes... to ensure their domination over the working class, thus enabling the former to subject the latter to the process of surplus-value extortion (i.e. to capitalist exploitation)' (ibid., p. 137). In this depiction the State is a 'Repressive State Apparatus' consisting of police, courts, prisons, the army and other institutions of 'repressive execution and intervention' 'in the interest of the ruling classes' (ibid.). Certainly, the Repressive State Apparatus plays a role in maintaining the *status quo* and with it the relations of production. The superstructural level of the legal-political is clustered around this state apparatus (albeit not identical with it). But Althusser adds something to this reductive Marxist theory of the state, namely the concept of *Ideological State Apparatuses.*

While the Repressive State Apparatus functions mainly by way of violence, the Ideological State Apparatuses (ISAs) function predominantly through ideology. Predominantly does not mean exclusively; the army and the police also function by means of ideology, while the educational ISA disciplines, punishes and teaches with practices that include manifold forms of violence. Another difference is that there is only one repressive apparatus but a multitude of ISAs,[4] which are 'distinct, "relatively autonomous" and capable of providing an objective field to contradictions which express... the effects of the clashes between the capitalist class struggle and the proletarian class struggle, as well as their subordinate forms' (ibid., p. 149). In their multiplicity they are unified under the *ruling ideology.* The last thing we will say about the repressive apparatus is that it secures, by (violent) repression, the political conditions for the ISAs. Althusser's hypothesis, we can now say, is that in their diversity the ISAs ultimately have a shared role, namely the reproduction of relations of production, i.e. the capitalist relations of exploitation they largely secure.

Rather than presenting the role and function of a specific ISA (the text discusses the religious and the educational ISAs, for instance), we will concern ourselves solely with the theory of *ideology in general.* Such a theory is possible, because '*ideology has no history*' (Althusser 2014a, p. 174). Marx made the same assertion in *The German Ideology,*[5] but meant something quite different (ideology is an illusion and only the material conditions that are reflected in that illusion have a history). What Althusser is aiming at is that in its basic functioning, ideology is *omni-historical, eternal* and *omni-present* in its immutable form throughout history (cf. Ibid., pp. 161ff.). There are innumerable ideolog*ies* that all have a history, i.e. are not eternal, but no social formation can exist *without* ideology. In *For Marx,* he writes:

[H]istorical materialism cannot conceive that even a communist society could ever do without ideology... it is not conceivable that communism, a new mode of production and relations of production, could do without a social organization of production, and corresponding ideological forms. (Althusser 1969, p. 232)

In every conceivable social formation, individuals have to 'find their place,' take up a subject position, make intelligible to themselves the conditions they exist in, and *live* their relation to those conditions. If ideology is thus eternal—a mechanism that is at work whenever individuals enter into associations with other individuals and produce their material life in definite conditions of production—trying to critique it as simply *false* consciousness is futile. Three main theses of Althusser's theory of ideology in general can be distilled from his text on ideology and ideological state apparatuses. They are: (I) *Ideology represents the imaginary relationship of individuals to their real conditions of existence.* (II) *It has a material existence.* (III) *Ideology interpellates individuals as subjects.*

I

The kind of ideology Marx and Engels put forward in *The German Ideology* is, for Althusser, 'an imaginary assemblage (*bricolage*), a pure dream, empty and vain, constituted by the "day's residues" from the only full and positive reality, that of concrete material individuals materially producing their existence' (Althusser 1972, p. 160). In other words, it is an imaginary representation of their real conditions. For the young Marx, the *cause* of the inversion that gives the representation an illusory character is not to be found in a conspiracy of powerful individuals indoctrinating the 'people' for their benefit, justifying their exploitation as natural. Rather, it lies in the material conditions themselves. Because the conditions are *alienating*, their representations are alienated (*false*) as well. To this, it seems, Althusser replies that:

it is not their real conditions of existence, their real world, that 'men' 'represent to themselves' in ideology, but above all it is their relation to those conditions of existence which is represented to them there. It is this relation which is at the center of every ideological, i.e. imaginary, representation of the real world. It is this relation that contains the 'cause' which has to explain the imaginary distortion of the ideological representation of the real world. (Althusser 1972, p. 164)

There are several reasons for Althusser's rejection of the 'Marxian' definition of ideology and his counter-proposal to see it as the 'representation of the *imaginary relationship* of individuals to their real conditions of existence,' as I see it.

The first reason concerns the idea of *alienation*. Very truncated, it can be summarized as the assertion that there is an early Marx and a later Marx, the former being a humanist influenced by Feuerbach and Hegel, the latter being the mature Marx of *Capital*. The humanist Marx adhered to the fallacy that there is a human essence and only through this could he assert that there is something essential, original, innate that humans can be *alienated* from. With essentialist humanism, we should abandon the concept of alienation. Without the concept of alienation as the cause of the illusory inversion, the proposition of ideology as the 'imaginary representation of real conditions' vanishes.

The second reason touches the problem of *representation* of real conditions. The social *structure* (mode of production) is, as we have seen, an *absent cause*. The structural effectivity of the real conditions of existence—'the structure, which is merely a specific combination of its peculiar elements, is nothing outside its effects' (Althusser and Balibar 1997, p. 189)—makes it impossible to represent them symbolically.[6] While ideology generally maintains that such a representation is possible, what can be represented in ideological practice is *the relationship* of individuals to their real conditions of existence. This *relationship* is necessarily imaginary.

The third reason involves Althusser's notion of *subjection*, i.e. that in and through ideology individuals are interpellated as subjects. *As subjects*, individuals practice the rituals of ideological recognition (we encounter each other as subjects and mutually display our recognition of this fact), which guarantees for them that they are, in fact, 'concrete, individual, distinguishable and (naturally) irreplaceable subjects' (Althusser 1972, p. 173). The subject representing their relationship with their conditions of existence does not exist before or outside of ideology, making the relationship a necessarily imaginary one. It is the relationship of subjects subjected to ideology that is represented. There are no individuals who could correctly represent their relationship but are then later turned into subjects by the distorting force of ideology. We are all always-already subjects.

Denoting ideology in this way indicates that individuals relate to their material conditions of existence in a necessarily distorted fashion. Those conditions include and are to a large part the relations of production that individuals enter independently of their will. Thus, 'all ideology represents in its necessarily imaginary distortion not the existing relations of production, but above all the (imaginary) relationship of individuals to the relations of production and the relations that derive from them' (ibid., p. 165). This is the first step to understanding the role ideology plays in the reproduction of those relations.

II

The term 'representation' has just been employed several times, yet it remains undefined. It was equivocated with the 'representation' in the 'imaginary representations of real conditions' in Marx, where it means, first and foremost, *ideas*. In fact, in *The German Ideology* and the *Brumaire* ideology appeared as consisting largely of ideas—mental representations— and their limitations. Yet, the ideas and representations that constitute ideology in the Althusserian sense 'do not have an ideal (*idéale* or *idée-lle*) or a spiritual existence, but a material existence' (Althusser 1972, p. 165). The representations of ideology are material because ideology exists in *material practices*. Concretely, they exist in the practices of the ISAs, where each apparatus is the realization of a specific ideology (unified with the other ideologies by their subjection to the ruling ideology). Even more specifically, they are to be found within the single parts of an apparatus inhabited by the individual at a given moment—for example 'a small mass at church, a funeral, a minor match at a sports' club, a school day, a political party meeting, etc.' (ibid., p. 168). The materiality of ideas in the practice(s) of an Ideological State Apparatus is best grasped as a *materiality of performative practices*. Ideas (including beliefs, convictions, etc.) need to be inscribed into the actions of practices in order to exist in a meaningful sense.

We can approach this congruence of ideas and practices from a commonsensical—that is, ideological—angle. The *ideological* attitude towards the connection between actions and ideas can be presented as follows: An individual believes in something (God, gender equality, the ethical superiority of organic vegetables…) and this belief comes from the inner depths of the individual's consciousness and is *really* their belief. Because we are all free autonomous subjects, individuals will (and should) obviously act according to their beliefs. If they believe that only prayer can give them salvation, they should pray. Otherwise they do not really believe (or something is wrong with them). In this *ideological* view the concurrence between (immaterial) idea and (material) action is still completely 'normative' but it recognizes that 'the "ideas" of a human subject exist in [their] actions' (ibid., p. 168). Althusser inverts this view with an allusion to Pascal who wrote:

> For we must make no mistake about ourselves: we are as much automaton as mind... Proofs only convince the mind; habit provides the strongest proofs and those that are most believed. It inclines the automaton, which leads the mind unconsciously with it. (Pascal 1966, p. 274)

The famous paraphrase of this quote ('Kneel down, move your lips in prayer, and you will believe') lies at the center of Althusser's concept of ideology. Real belief is external; ideas are material actions; the reality of a conviction is *performative*. Moreover, ideas and representations do not evolve out of the subject's transcendental consciousness as in Kant, but are *derived* from the ideological apparatuses that enable the subject to position itself in (material) social reality.

There seems to be no haven for the immaterial in this materialist conception of ideas and consciousness. There is simply a multitude of manners of not being ideational. When Althusser says that, when a single subject is concerned, 'the existence of the ideas of his belief is material in that *his ideas are his material actions inserted into material practices governed by material rituals which are themselves defined by the material ideological apparatus from which derive the ideas of that subject*' (Althusser 1972, p. 169), we are confronted with modes of materiality that range from beliefs, actions, practices to rituals and apparatuses.[7] Althusser recognizes this ('Of course, the material existence of the ideology in an apparatus and its practices does not have the same modality as the material existence of a paving-stone or a rifle' (ibid., p. 166)) but he does not spell out the modalities of materiality he refers to. At this juncture it will suffice to say that it is not the *mental, immaterial* relation to real conditions and relations that matters in ideology but the *real* 'lived' relation.[8] Individuals do not just *think* ideology, they '"live" their ideologies as the Cartesian "saw" or did not see—if he was not looking at it—the moon two hundred paces away: *not at all as a form of consciousness, but as an object of their "world"*—as their *"world"* itself' (Althusser 1969, p. 233). The materiality of ideology is, furthermore, tied to the apparatuses. Thus, it is quite differ-ent from the material practices that constitute *commodity fetishism*. There is a difference 'between the *materiality that always-already pertains to ideology as such* (material, effective apparatuses which give body to ideol-ogy) and *ideology that always-already pertains to materiality as such* (to the social actuality of production)' (Žižek 2012, pp. 10–11).

To the attestation that ideology exists in material practices, Althusser adds that there is no practice except by and in ideology. To *practically* live the relation to their conditions of existence, the individual has to be an ideological subject. Without ideology there is action and movement, but no *practice*. And there is no practice and no ideology except by the subject and for subjects.

III

This last point takes us to Althusser's final proposition:

> [T]here is no ideology except by the subject and for subjects. Meaning, there is no ideology except for concrete subjects, and this destination for ideology is only made possible by the subject: meaning, *by the category of the subject* and its functioning. (Althusser and Balibar 1997, p. 169)

The subject is constitutive *of* ideology and constituted *by* ideology. You and I always-already are subjects and unless you are reading this as a lin-guist or a sociologist, it is almost always completely obvious that we are. Just by recognizing that it *could* be you that is meant, you are entering the 'rituals of ideological recognition' (Althusser 1972, p. 169). We live, talk, think, 'have our being' *in* ideology; it is the *Logos* we move in. The text's use of that term[9] is certainly no coincidence, and it is crucial to the constitution of the subject. It, for the first time in our investigation, brings forward the dimension of the *symbolic* to the theories of ideology and the subject in Marxist thinking. In anticipation of the next chapter, ideology can be seen as material *discourse* in which the relations between the indi-viduals are symbolically defined. In a short text found in his correspon-dence, published posthumously, and just recently translated, Althusser writes that 'in order for the individual to be constituted as an interpel-lated subject, it must recognize itself as a subject in ideological discourse' (Althusser 2014b, p. 87). This concurrently opens up the conceptualiza-tions of subject and ideology to the fields of meaning and signification.

But how do individuals enter the *Symbolic Order* that is ideology? By ideology *interpellating 'concrete individuals as concrete subjects'* (Althusser 1972, p. 173), Althusser says. It is the *function*[10] of ideology to constitute subjects and outside of this (material, practical) function ideology does not exist. *Interpellation,* or *hailing*, is the operation by which ideology 'recruits' concrete individuals as subjects and can be imagined on the lines of someone calling ('hey, you!' or whistling, or gesturing, or provid-ing a material *sign*) an individual, who recognizes that 'the hail was "really" addressed to him, and that "it was *really him* who was hailed" (and not someone else)' (ibid., p. 174). It is a (signifying) *practice* embedded in rituals of ideological recognition that presupposes ideological subjects to work. This presupposition, apart from underlining that we always-already are subjects, draws attention to two questions: 'What is the difference between subject and individual?' and 'When does an individual become a subject?'

The individual is the singular biological-material support of the subject. It is an *abstract* category, even if it is a *concrete* individual (possessing a material body). It is abstract, because—again—it is always-already a sub-ject: even the unborn child possesses a *'pre-natal sociality,'* or better yet, a projected fetal subject position since it is 'appointed as a subject in and by the specific familial ideological configuration in which it is "expected" once it is conceived' (ibid., p. 176). The problems this assertion raises are obvious. What is distinct about the subject if even the fetus fits the category? How can the distinction be maintained if we are all always both at the same time (you cannot tell the individual and the subject apart by looking at them)?

In Lacanian psychoanalysis, which is something Althusser leans heavily on, the infant enters the Imaginary *at a specific time.* The *'thou art that'* of the *imaginary* relation to oneself, which is revealed in the mirror-stage of the child, occurs months after birth (cf. Lacan and Fink 2006, pp. 75–81). In Althusser's account there is no temporal sequence which would allow for writing the genealogy of a single individual that at some point is recruited as a subject by ideology. The simultaneous subjection and sub-jectivation of the concrete individual *happens* in the ideological practice of interpellation, but it does so without temporal succession: 'The existence of ideology and the hailing or interpellation of individuals as subjects are one and the same thing' (Althusser 1972, p. 176). Through interpellation the subject is designated a place in the social formation (ideology never happens outside of a social formation) that it has to (freely) accept and choose. Ideology keeps subjects in place.

How are ideology and subjectivation related to the reproduction of the relations of production? It was said that ideological practice is situated in a variety of ISAs that are, in their diversity, united under a ruling ideology—the ideology of the ruling class. Consequently, in every ISA, no matter how divergent the various ISAs are from each other, the dominant ideology is transmitted, performed, institutionalized. As the ideology of the ruling class, it is an ideology that secures the relations of production. Thus, while ideology is no longer construed as *false consciousness*, a part of social reality exists that is necessarily distorted in the imaginary relationships of individuals to their real conditions of existence: 'The reality which is necessarily *ignored* (*méconnue*)... is indeed, in the last resort, the reproduction of the relations of production and the relations deriving from it' (ibid., pp. 182–183). The *material* relations of production affect the subject structurally through subjectivation and subjection in and by the ideology which, in the last analysis, secures those relations.

Ideology, understood as the mechanism by which individuals are interpellated as subjects, is universal for Althusser. General though his theory may be, it is nonetheless worthwhile to touch upon a few aspects of his concept that appear to be more or less specific to capitalism. For one, the concept of the *subject* is a relatively recent one, starting its rise with bourgeois legal practice. The eternity of ideology therefore depends on Althusser's claim that the *category* of the subject has existed under different names throughout history (e.g. as 'the soul' in Plato). This equivalence can surely be doubted. As can the assumption of a dominant ideology. How would dominant ideologies arise in a social formation without (class) domination? If ideology is the representation of an imaginary relationship to real conditions and can be compared to Freud's equally eternal *Unconscious* (which is what Althussser does), then the question of how a different social organization would affect the very structure of ideology remains unanswered. There might even be *right* consciousness in changed material conditions (which is the more Marxian position). What would be effective as ideology in *communism* might only bear a family resemblance to the forms of ideology in *capitalism,* merely denoting the mechanism by which subjects imagine their relation to their social formation. The universality of ideology and its apparatuses should, therefore, not be over-extended.

The de-historization of the type of subject that is implicated in Althusser's theory of ideology may be regarded as another problem. His theory denies the possibility of an autonomous and centered subject, not just in capitalism but also in the past and future. For Althusser, 'such a subject never existed in the first place but constituted something like an ideological mirage' (Jameson 1991, p. 15). The historical contingency of forms of subjectivity is thus halted, albeit at a very basic level that allows for different subjectivities to arise from the fundamental subjection to the general mechanism of ideology. What should be considered in a theory of the subject is, then, something Jameson calls a 'reality of appearance' (ibid.). In the past it might have *really* appeared as though the subject was more 'centered' and autonomous than in late capitalism. A subject, that is, not subjected to the process of reification, relating to other subjects in relations not colonized by the logic of exchange and *Verdinglichung* (reification).

Generally, the specific ideolog*ies* that interpellate individuals as subjects are subject to radical change throughout history. While subjects cannot escape ideology in general, specific ideologies can be criticized and their causes potentially identified. This is true, be they political, ethical, or religious—like that of a virgin giving birth to a boy that is at the same time his own father, who then gets sacrificed by God (who he himself is) for the sins of people that are all ancestors of a man created from dirt and a women made from a rib who ate an evil fruit because a talking snake told them to. The field of ideology is a field of struggle between ideologies striving for dominance or 'hegemony.' It is therefore also a field in which *subjectivities* are constructed and institutionalized. With this being said, what is the subject in Althusser's theory of ideology?

The subject is neither center nor origin. It is not pure consciousness and it is neither unified nor autonomous. The subject implicated in the theory of ideology brought forward here bears fundamental differences to the idealist conceptions that were introduced in the *Prelude,* without, however, amounting to a simplistic dismissal of the category altogether.

By virtue of its dependence on interpellation (1) the subject is invariably *social,* depending on *inter*subjective, symbolic processes and signifying practices that are the prerequisite of identity and subjectivity. It is thus not a monadic, *singular* subject. (2) It is constituted by social forces that lie outside it. Although it constitutes an element of the social formation that conditions it, the subject is by no means the single *origin* of the world it inhabits. (3) The subject's ideas, beliefs, practices *all* have their existence in ideology and cannot be prescinded from material discourses and institutions—such as the Ideological State Apparatuses—from which ideas etc. are *derived*. Not only is the subject not the origin of the world, it is not the origin of thoughts and actions, either. The subject is (4) not *unified* and *centered*. Its practical engagement in multiple ISAs decenters it and renders it the site of contradictory and conflicting 'ideas' and knowledges. The multiple ideolog*ies* of the apparatuses are, while unified under the ruling ideology, by no means uniform. The numerous ISAs a subject is practically engaged in can contradict and stand in opposition to each other. In an individual ISA, then, subjects are interpellated and recognize their interpellation, thus 'it obtains from them the *recognition* that they really do occupy the place it designates for them and theirs in the world, a fixed residence' (Althusser 1972, p. 178). Ideology positions, places, or, alternatively, offers subject-positions to the subject that can only then enter the necessarily imaginary relation to its real conditions of existence. It is, in that sense, (5) not free. Furthermore the subject is subjected to a *Subject*, akin to Lacan's big Other. In the respective ISAs, the subject is *subjected* to the *Subject* (God, democracy, football, morale…) of that ISA. Like the subject of Kant's ethics, to be a free subject the individual has to subject themself to a Subject. He (or she) is

> *interpellated as a (free) subject in order that he shall submit freely to the commandments of the Subject, i.e. in order that he shall (freely) accept his subjection,* i.e. in order he shall make the gestures and actions of his subjection 'all by himself.' *There are no subjects except by and for their subjection.* That is why they 'work all by themselves.' (Althusser 1972, p. 182)[11]

In its subordination and subjection (6) the subject is *subiectus* and not *hypokmeímenon, subiectum*. The subject is subjected in *material* institutions through *material* practices embedded in *material* rituals, which 'ideas' are derivative of. Furthermore, *material* ideology functions to secure the reproduction of *material* relations of production—meaning that the subject is entirely constituted by material reality. A reality, nevertheless, that is produced by subjects and is collectively controlled by them.

Materiality Without Matter? The 'Material' in Marxism

In Marxist materialism, the 'material' is not reducible to physical, tangible matter. Rather, materiality refers to that which is not ideational. What is *material,* is thus defined negatively. I will, however, suggest that *within* this negative characterization of materiality, several positive materialities can be identified. This amounts to the proposition that there are several modalities of materiality—several modes of *not being ideational*.

Classical materialism 'posits the primitive unicity of being' and gives the multiplicity that constitutes this unity a name: *matter;* that is, in the narrow sense, 'mass, electrons, atoms, energy, waves, various particles, and so on' (Badiou 2013, p. 190). In addition, materialism asserts the *primacy* of the material over the ideal or ideational. An inversion of idealism that simply puts matter in the place of the idea, and thereby replaces one *interpretative* principle with another, is what Marx termed 'old' materialism. Such materialism not only disregards practical human activity, but in its reversal also perpetuates the ontological dualism of *being* and *consciousness*. In Marx, the idea is not substituted by immutable *matter,* instead the concept of *practice* is introduced as a corrective to the contemplative attitude towards material reality. As a theory of practice, Marxism emphasizes the processual and practical *production* of material conditions and thereby disencumbers the latter from their status as a natural force that individuals have no control over. Practical human activity is, however, not *identical* with what Marx denotes as material. Material *conditions*, material *reality*, material *production*, material *relations* etc. are all not synonymous with practice.

There has been disagreement in Marxist theory about what kind of materiality it is that Marx refers to. Alain Badiou, for instance, insists on a non-mechanical, dialectical materialism of *matter* that distinguishes matter and (material) thought as regions of being, with the first ruling over the second (cf. Badiou 2013, pp. 190–196). Fredric Jameson argues for a *historical* materialism, which is not mechanical and not primarily concerned with matter,[12] but 'insists on an ultimate determination by the mode of production,' and he furthermore remarks 'that the grounding of materialism in one or another conception of matter is rather the hallmark of bourgeois ideology from the eighteenth-century materialisms all the way down to nineteenth-century positivism and determinism' (Jameson 2002, p. 30). Balibar claims that Marx's is a 'materialism without matter' that has its name 'in order to *take the contrary stance to that of idealism*' (Balibar 2007, p. 23). Or Jakubowski, who is certain that 'for Marx, the material is the *sensuously* real, something whose reality does not exist only in consciousness' (Jakubowski 1990, p. 23). These are arbitrary examples; nevertheless they show that there is some diversity in how to understand materiality in Marxist thinking. At the same time, all four authors can be said to *highlight* particular aspects of the materiality implicit in Marxist materialism.

Material conditions possess their materiality first of all by their being 'real,' which is just another way of saying 'not ideal.' 'Material' in Marx's writings often connotes just that; it is the *other* of the idea. The phenomena subsumed under this negative delineation can, however, be *conceptually* separated so as to present them as modalities of materiality, although they obviously overlap.

1. There is, for one, the *positive materiality of matter*. This modality contains things like bodies, food, clothes, tools, buildings, smartphones and all manner of artifacts. Tanks, machine-guns, banknotes and texts are positively material, as are the vibrating air currents of spoken language. They consist of particles, atoms, molecules, waves, and come close to what a physicist would call 'material.' All those material entities are elements of material conditions and no Marxist would deny their materiality. Additionally, 'nature'—climate, weather, geological formations, etc.—could be included in this modality. Yet, while a flood is definitely material and can alter conditions of living and producing, humans *transform* nature.[13] The same could be said of other materialities of this modality. They are *matter* in the strictest sense. However, following our discussion of Marxian materialism it should be evident that such materialities of matter cannot be understood as isolated objects of passive contemplation or determining forces abstracted from human activity—this was the fallacy of the old materialisms.

   Although this modality is partly comprised of 'things,' within a materialist dialectic these things must be recognized simultaneously as objects and as processes. The 'matter' of this modality of materiality is thus quite different from both the 'vibrant,' enchanted matter of New Materialism and the solid, tangible matter of certain more deterministic or 'scientistic' strands of materialism.

2. The stress on *processes* we have encountered in the preceding chapters points to a second modality of materiality. It is not only *tangible* objects that are material but also *processes* and *practices*. This modality could be understood as a materiality of *displacement,* or *mutability*. Practices are not merely material because they are supported by bodies and artifacts; their materiality also resides in their efficacy of *changing* aspects of the material world. The practice of production *transforms* all entities involved (raw material, tools, producer, product).

Processes by definition transform and/or displace the elements involved in them—change that does not take place in some immaterial realm. Furthermore, practices and processes are generally observable and describable. Therefore practical human activity that produces conditions of production is a *material* process.

3. The third kind of materiality implicit in Marxist theory can best be described as the materiality of *objectivity* or *effectivity*. It encompasses social relations, such as relations of production, and institutions like ISAs as well as the institution of the dichotomy of genders, which has a material reality. But it also includes 'social facts,' rules, or beliefs that exert an *objective* force on individuals. In short: everything that has *facticity* and makes an objective difference.

Such materialities of *effectivity* are necessarily entwined with and reliant upon processes, practices, and matter of some sort. For instance, the reliance of social relations on ideological practice and other material support was evidenced in the present chapter when Althusser's theory of ideology was presented.

This classification, inexhaustive as it may be, will have served its purpose as long as it has made one thing clear: The 'material' in Marxist materialism is more than *matter* or *matter in motion*.

Although more modes of being material will be presented, the claim that materiality is always more than solid matter is something behind which we will not regress in the following chapters. We will now turn to another family of theories, in which the subject is decentered by material instances largely elided thus far—namely language, discourse and their fundamental materiality.

NOTES

1. '[T]he economic dialectic is never active in the pure state; in History, these instances, the superstructures, etc.—are never seen to step respectfully aside when their work is done or, when the Time comes, as his pure phenomena, to scatter before His Majesty the Economy as he strides along the royal road of the Dialectic' (Althusser 1969, p. 113).

2. For a discussion of this important field, see e.g. Vogel et al. (2013) and Federici (2012).

3. What is necessary to reproduce labor power is not 'biological', but historically contingent. Althusser quotes Marx as saying that 'English workers need beer while French proletarians need wine' (ibid., p. 131). A TV,

internet, a mobile phone, more than two pairs of underwear could all be said to be included in today's western 'historically variable minimum.' Generally, the minimum is determined in good old class struggle.

4. He names 'the religious ISA (the system of the different Churches), the educational ISA (the system of the different public and private "Schools"), the family ISA, the legal ISA, the political ISA (the political system, including the different parties), the trade union ISA, the communications ISA (press, radio and television, etc,), the cultural ISA (Literature, the Arts, sports, etc.)' (Althusser 1972, p. 143). According to Althusser, the dominant ISA in mature capitalist formations is the educational ISA.

5. 'Morality, religion, metaphysics, all the rest of ideology and their corresponding forms of consciousness, thus no longer retain the semblance of independence. They have no history, no development; but men, developing their material production and their material intercourse, alter, along with this their real existence, their thinking and the products of their thinking' (Marx and Engels 1965, p. 38).

6. That capitalism as such is 'unrepresentable' is the problem Fredric Jameson devotes his book *Representing Capital* (Jameson 2011) to. Instead of concluding that 'since it is unrepresentable, capitalism is ineffable and a kind of mystery beyond language,' he proposes to 'redouble one's efforts to express the inaccessible in this respect' (ibid., p. 7).

7. Take the material practices governed by material rituals in the religious ISA: 'the materialities of displacement for going to mass, of kneeling down, of the gesture of the sign of the cross, or of the mea culpa, of a sentence, of a prayer, of an act of contribution, of a penitence, of a gaze, of a handshake, of an external verbal discourse or an "internal" verbal discourse (consciousness), are not one and the same materiality' (Althusser 1972, p. 169).

8. '[Ideology] is distinct from other social instances, but also that men live their actions, usually referred to freedom and "consciousness" by the classical tradition, in ideology, by and through ideology; in short, that the "lived" relation between men and the world, including History (in political action or inaction), passes through ideology, or better, is ideology itself' (Althusser 1969, p. 233).

9. He writes that 'as St Paul admirably put it, it is the "Logos," meaning ideology,' which we live in (Althusser 1972, p. 171).

10. Saying that ideology has a function might seem incommensurable with Althusser's anti-functionalist approach. I use it as he does, I think—as a shortcut to denote what it does. For a discussion of functionalism in Althusser's theory of ideology see also: Lock (1996, pp. 72ff).

11. Althusser's dictum of 'history without a subject and without a telos' is now much more easily understood. The subject alluded to is on the one hand Hegel's Subject with a capital 'S' that the subjects subject themselves to in

order to be 'free.' And on the other hand it is aimed at Lukács's proletariat as 'subject of history.' Neither of these subjects is compatible with the notion of history in Althusser's structural Marxism. See, for instance Jameson (2008, p. 112).

12. Which is not to say that he dismisses the material character of reality. For example, he writes that 'capitalism, and the modern age, is a period in which, with the extinction of the sacred and the "spiritual," the deep underlying materiality of all things has finally risen dripping and convulsive into the light of day' (Jameson 1991, p. 67).

13. Discussing materiality and nature in Marxism, Castree, to give an example, writes: 'By materiality I mean both the real, ontological existence and causal efficacy and agency within history, of those entities and processes we call "natural"' (Castree 1995, p. 20). Yet, what is 'natural' does not resemble untouched nature or natural laws. Godelier writes that 'of all the forces which set [humans] in movement and prompt them to invent new forms of society, the most profound is their ability to transform their relations with nature by transforming nature itself' (Godelier 2011, pp. 1–2).

References

Althusser, L. (1969). *For Marx*. New York: Pantheon Books.

Althusser, L. (1972). Ideology and ideological state apparatuses (notes towards an investigation). In L. Althusser (Ed.), *Lenin and philosophy, and other essays* (pp. 127–188). New York: Monthly Review Press.

Althusser, L. (2014a). *On the reproduction of capitalism: Ideology and ideological state apparatuses*. London: Verso.

Althusser, L. (2014b). Three notes on the theory of discourses. In J. Angermuller, D. Maingueneau, & R. Wodak (Eds.), *The discourse studies reader: Main currents in theory and analysis* (pp. 83–88). Amsterdam: John Benjamins Publishing.

Althusser, L., & Balibar, E. (1997). *Reading Capital*. London: Verso.

Badiou, A. (2013). *Theory of the subject*. London: Bloomsbury Academic.

Balibar, E. (2007). *The philosophy of Marx*. London: Verso.

Castree, N. (1995). The nature of produced nature: Materiality and knowledge production in Marxism. *Antipode, 27*(1), 12–48.

Federici, S. (2012). *Revolution at point zero: Housework, reproduction, and feminist struggle*. Oakland, CA: PM Press.

Godelier, M. (2011). *The mental and the material: Thought, economy, and society*. London: Verso.

Jakubowski, F. (1990). *Ideology and superstructure in historical materialism*. London: Pluto.

Jameson, F. (1991). *Postmodernism, or, the cultural logic of late capitalism*. London:

Verso.

Jameson, F. (2002). *The political unconscious: Narrative as a socially symbolic act.* London: Routledge.

Jameson, F. (2008). *The ideologies of theory.* London: Verso.

Jameson, F. (2011). *Representing capital: A commentary of volume one.* London: Verso.

Lacan, J., & Fink, B. (2006). *Ecrits.* New York: W.W. Norton & Co.

Lenin, V. I. (1975). *A new chapter of world history* (pp. 368–369). Moscow: Progress Publishers.

Lock, G. (1996). Subject, interpellation, and ideology. In A. Callari, D. F. Ruccio, & L. Althusser (Eds.), *Postmodern materialism and the future of Marxist theory: Essays in the Althusserian tradition* (pp. 69–90). Hanover: Wesleyan University Press.

Marx, K., & Engels, F. (1965). *The German ideology.* London: Lawrence & Wishart.

Pascal, B. (1966). *Pensées.* Harmondsworth: Penguin.

Vogel, L., Ferguson, S., & McNally, D. (2013). *Marxism and the oppression of women: Toward a unitary theory.* Chicago, IL: Haymarket Books.

Žižek, S. (2012). The sprectre of ideology. In S. Žižek (Ed.), *Mapping ideology* (pp. 1–33). London: Verso.

CHAPTER 5

The Materiality of Language and the Decentered Subject

Abstract Language and discourse are fundamentally material and the subject is constituted and decentered in relation to this materiality. It is the theories emerging from structuralism that dealt most thoroughly with the relation between material language and subjectivity. After giving a brief introduction to Saussure's structural linguistics and the diverse assemblage of writers often labeled 'post-structuralists,' the chapter discusses the materialities of language and discourse as they were conceptualized by Bachtin, Barthes, Derrida, Kristeva, and others. In the second part, different post-structuralist approaches to the constitution and decentering of the subject in material language and discourse are presented.

Keywords Post-structuralism • Materiality of language • Discourse • Subjectivity • Subject position

In Marxist theory—at least until the middle of the last century—language was a kind of blind spot that did not seem to deserve much attention. Apart from Vološinov's pioneering work in *Marxism and the Philosophy of Language* and Marr's failed attempt to explain language as a superstructural phenomenon that is formed by economic conditions, genuinely Marxist theories of language were rare. In 1950 Stalin denounced Marr's linguistics, and *Marxism and the Problems of Linguistics* (Stalin 1972) was published. In it, Stalin states that language is not simply 'superstructural' but

J. Beetz, *Materiality and Subject in Marxism, (Post-)Structuralism, and Material Semiotics*, DOI 10.1057/978-1-137-59837-0_5

he does not develop anything remotely resembling a materialist philosophy of language.[1] The (post-)structuralist theories we will be concerned with now would later inform Marxist thinkers' (such as Žižek, Eagleton, or Leclercle) ideas about ideology and the subject. The subject is, for them, 'not only interpellated by ideology… but subjectified by the language that speaks it' (Leclercle 2006, p. 165). The subject is, then, not only constituted in relation to material conditions but also in and through language and discourse. In the following chapter, we will discuss how theoretical approaches that are usually called '(post-)structuralist' conceptualize *the materiality of language* as well as the construction of the subject in this materiality.

The fundamental materiality of language and discourse has generally been disregarded with a surprising consistency and does not figure too prominently in the current discussions revolving around materiality and the New Materialisms.[2] Still, the theories presented are certainly not the only approaches to acknowledge the material character of linguistic and signifying phenomena. Silverman and Torode, for instance, wrote extensively on the materiality of language without being easily classified as (post-)structuralists (cf. Silverman and Torode 1980). In Germany, Sybille Krämer (e.g. Krämer 2001, pp. 270ff.), Friedrich Kittler (e.g. Kittler 1988, 1990), and Hans-Ulrich Gumbrecht (1988) are examples of thinkers who theorize language as material. Equally, there are other *materialist* conceptualizations of language that will not be dealt with in this chapter. To name just two of those, Wittgenstein (2001) as well as Austin (1962) could be said to have developed materialist philosophies of language, albeit without being concerned with the latter's materiality.

The influence of language on the formation of subjectivity, meanwhile, has been a theme in the philosophy of language for almost two centuries (cf., e.g. Humboldt 1988, pp. 56ff.). Sociolinguistics (see, e.g. Edwards 2009) and linguistic anthropology (e.g. Duranti 1997) equally understand subjectivity, identity, 'consciousness,' etc. as *conditioned* by language. Yet, in those philosophies and theories language is hardly ever understood as *material*. The broad field of theories that emerged from structuralism, however, is where the relation between material language and the subject (or what takes its place) was thought through most thoroughly.[3]

To understand (post-)structuralism, the materiality of language, and its role in the constitution and decentering of the subject we will start at the beginning: with Saussure's structural linguistics. After giving an overview of the developments of structuralism and post-structuralism, language is presented in its multiple materiality, drawing on the typology of materialities developed in the preceding chapters. In a next step, the discussion around the 'death of the author' is briefly recounted to then turn to some approaches to the subject and its constitution in ideological and discursive practices of *positioning*.

SAUSSURE'S STRUCTURAL LINGUISTICS

When we speak, we do not communicate *meaning*, we communicate *language*. This simple assertion constitutes the starting point of Saussure's semiology. Language, for him, consists of *signs*. Linguistic signs, however, do not unite a name and a thing; they are not words that somehow correspond to the things they name. Rather, a *sign* unites 'a concept and a sound-image,' that is, a 'psychological imprint' (de Saussure 1986, p. 66) of a material sound and the mental concept evoked by that sound-image. The sound-image is called the *signifier*, the concept or mental image is designated the *signified*. These two 'sides' of the sign are intimately linked and cannot be divided. The signs in language are like a piece of paper— the *signifier* being one side, the *signified* the other. And just like a piece of paper 'one cannot cut the front without cutting the back at the same time,' meaning 'one can neither divide sound from thought nor thought from sound' (ibid., p. 113). *Signifier* and *signified*, united as they may be in the *sign*, are only connected *arbitrarily*. There is no *necessary* connection, no intrinsic link, between a sound-image like [dolphin] and the mental image of 'dolphin' evoked by it. That makes the whole *sign* arbitrary, resting on nothing but social convention.

The arbitrariness of the connection between *signifiers* and *signifieds* also transforms the whole of language into a structure without positive terms—without fixed meaning. Thus Saussure writes that in language 'there are only differences *without positive terms*. Whether we take the signified or the signifier, language has neither ideas nor sounds that existed before the linguistic system, but only conceptual and phonic differences that have issued from the system' (ibid., p. 120). The *value* of a sign is exclusively determined by its difference from other signs. Thence, a *sign* or a word does not have an original, intrinsic meaning: instead meaning is produced through differences and relations. Like in a game of chess, where a knight can be replaced with a piece of wax without changing the value of the newly dubbed knight or the rules of the game, in language the value of a sign is independent of the form the sign takes. What matters is its difference to the other elements in the language system in which those elements 'hold each other in equilibrium in accordance with fixed rules' (ibid., p. 110).

That signs refer to each other rather than to things *outside* of language introduces the problem of reference in Saussurean semiology. There are the material vehicle of the *signifier* and the meaning of the *signified*, but there is also a 'third component—the external object of the sign, its reference or "referent"' which does not take part in the play of signs and is 'henceforth expelled from the unity, yet haunting it as a ghostly residual aftereffect' (Jameson 2008, p. 502). What the *signifier* signifies is not the object it names, but the mental image it elicits. Consequently, if the relationship internal to the sign (*signifier* and *signified*) is arbitrary, the connection between sign and referent is similarly severed.

In spite of signs' arbitrary character, they still *work*. Evidently it is possible to communicate through signs. That the functioning depends on *convention* and *agreement* indicates the ultimately *social* reality of language. No language can exist outside a community of speakers (or writers), or better yet, there can be no *realization* of language without such a community. The differentiation of language and realized language pertains to another foundational distinction in Saussure's linguistics, namely that between *langue* and *parole*.

The signifying system and its rules, thus described as a structure of signs, is what Saussure calls *langue*. *Langue* stands opposed to *parole*, which names the innumerable utterances and written actualizations of language. Containing the principles and conventionalized rules for signification, the abstract *langue* is the prerequisite for *meaningful* utterances in actualized *parole*. More so, *langue* is the precondition for *understanding parole*. For Saussure, the systematic, scientific analysis of *parole* is impossible. Although *langue* does not exist outside its realization in speech and writing and can only be investigated through the study of *parole* (e.g. 'by testing the limits and characteristic forms of any native speaker's understanding' (Jameson 1974, p. 26)), *parole* itself resists systematization. The totality of different ways actual people actually use words (intone them, use them in different contexts, combine them) is simply not comprehensible for a scientist—there are millions of ways to speak in a language. Semiology can, however, theorize and analyze *langue*.

Any language system associated with a community of speakers inevitably changes over time, and these changes can be observed and analyzed by linguists. Incidentally, this is what Saussure did in his early 'neo-grammarian' writings. In his *Course in General Linguistics*,[4] however, he abandons the *diachronic* view on language for a *synchronic* perspective that analyzes language as a system of signs at *one* point in time. For Saussure, approaching language synchronically means insisting on the fact that language is *complete* at any one point in time and does not evolve teleologically to a more 'adequate,' 'perfect' system of signs. Language is, then, 'a perpetual present, with all the possibilities of meaning implicit in its every moment' (ibid., p. 6). The synchronic approach thus stands opposed to philosophies of language that see their object of study as *deficient* in its capacity to express internal states or communicate external events.

The exclusion of diachronic thinking which results from Saussure's semiology makes the latter a-historical. While he does not deny the historical change of language systems and acknowledges social forces influencing this change over time (cf. de Saussure 1986, p. 78) his aim is to account not for development but for fundamental principles of a structure examined frozen in time.

As a structure of linguistic signs, language is but *one* signifying system. Saussure's structural linguistics is, according to him, only a part of the general science of semiology, which is the '*science that studies the life of signs within society*' (ibid., p. 16). Semiology thus includes the study of *all* signifying practices and systems in a society. As we will see in a moment, structuralism after Saussure embraced the study of 'the life of signs within society,' but rather than relegating linguistics to the fringe of semiology, language would become the model for all signifying structures.

THE METAPHOR OF LANGUAGE

Saussure's linguistics, together with Marxism and Freudian psychoanalysis, set the foundation for the development of structuralism and the subsequent emergence of so-called post-structuralism, or Theory. Any enumeration of theorists classed together under either one of these terms (but especially post-structuralism) calls for the figurative figleaf of assuring the reader that the author is aware of the inadmissibility of such a grouping. Still, (post-)structuralism is widely understood to encompass writers as diverse as Louis Althusser, Roland Barthes, Judith Butler, Gilles Deleuze, Jacques Derrida, Michel Foucault, Algirdas Julien Greimas, Felix Guattari, Luce Irigaray, Julia Kristeva, Jacques Lacan, Claude Lévi-Strauss, Michel Serres, and many others.

What unites them in their differences is their relationship with structural linguistics—they either critique it from the perspective of their respective disciplines or incorporate and transfer elements of structural linguistics into their field of study, or both. In France, where most of the aforementioned authors lived, the term 'post-structuralism' is not in use[5] and neither would the authors themselves necessarily have felt themselves part of an intellectual movement with that name. Thus, 'the reactions of French intellectuals tend to range from astonishment to irritation when they hear their international colleagues talk of "French poststructuralism"' (Angermuller 2015, p. 2).

It can, however, be maintained that at the beginning of the second half of the last century, there was an increase in work in the humanities that was 'based on the metaphor or model of a linguistic system' (Jameson 1974, p. ix). The general trend in the humanities and social sciences to turn to language was not limited to 'structuralist' works, but included, for example, developments in philosophy (Austin, Kripke, Russell, Searle, Wittgenstein, *et al.*). These developments came to be known as the *linguistic turn*.[6]

For the more structuralist thinkers of that time, language—as it was conceptualized by Saussure—became the framework in which they devised their theories and methods. The scope of this appropriation of structural linguistic vocabulary and method reached from anthropology (e.g. Lévi-Strauss 1963) over literary and cultural theory (e.g. Barthes 1972) to psychoanalysis (e.g. Lacan and Fink 2006). Coward and Ellis, referring to this *linguistic turn*, write that perhaps 'the most significant feature of twentieth-century intellectual development has been the way in which the study of language has opened the route to an understanding of mankind, social history and the laws of how a society functions' (Coward and Ellis 1977, p. 1).

Old problems endemic to the humanities and social sciences could now be re-examined by subjecting them to the structuralist method. Not only could linguistic signifying systems be analyzed anew; also non-linguistic structures were analyzed *in terms of* or as *comparable to* the structure of language. Lévi-Strauss and his studies on kinship structures are an example of structuralist thought.[7] Lacan's psychoanalysis and most famously his proclamation that 'the unconscious… is structured like a language' (Lacan and Fink 2006, p. 737) may serve as another prominent example of such transcoding. Furthermore, social *practices* could be conceived of as *signifying* practices and thus, as Kristeva states, the 'various manifestations of signifying acts were studied as *languages*. In this way were laid the bases for a scientific approach to the vast realm of human conditions' (Kristeva and Menke 1989, pp. 3–4). From this novel perspective, social phenomena appeared in a new light that illuminated not the essences of elements of the social, but their fundamental *relationality*. As in Saussure's linguistics, the significance of any one element was seen to lie in its *difference* to and *relationship* with all other elements in the *structure* it is a part of.

The notion that language does not designate the essences of things is not new. Already Nietzsche knew that a 'creator of language… only designates the relations between things and men, and to express them he resorts to the boldest metaphors' (Nietzsche 2009, p. 256) and that 'all these relations refer only to each other, and they are thoroughly incomprehensible to us in their essence' (Nietzsche 2009, p. 261). Earlier *even*, in Spinoza's system, what things are depends on their being *different* from other things rather than on something intrinsic.[8]

What was new, however, was the perspective on 'man' or 'the subject' that would emerge out of the structuralist endeavor as well as the metaphor of language that came with it. In structuralism, the speaking subject is no longer the origin of meaning. The subject thinks and experiences the world in *language*, a structure that precedes it. Thus, it seems, the subject is *spoken* by language as much as it *speaks* language.[9] The subject is now 'a function of a more impersonal system or language-structure' (Jameson 1974, pp. 134–135); it is constructed by the symbol. It is neither the center from which emanate language and practices nor the origin of meaning. The structuralist approach considers 'man' as language, which is not only the most radical moment of this approach, but 'putting language in the place of man constitutes the demystifying gesture par excellence' (Kristeva and Menke 1989, p. 4) as well.

The death (or at the very least the crisis) of the Cartesian subject in (post-)structuralist thinking resulted, among other things, from its decentering in language. Lacan's split subject, whose unconscious is structured like a language and which is always-already 'entangled in the pitfalls of the symbolic' (Angermuller 2014, p. 140) became the ensign of this development in post-Sartrean intellectual life in France. The notion of the subject's constitution in the symbolic order of language also makes Althusser's theory of ideology more readily intelligible. The *Logos* of ideology is inseparable from the *Logos* of language narrowly understood. It is this decentering of the subject as well as the role of *material* language in the deconstruction of the subject that we will be concerned with in this chapter.

Aside from the subject, *reference, representation*, and *meaning* have to be reconsidered if they are to be thought of in the structuralist framework. For anything to have meaning there must be a system of distinctions and conventions that forego the produced meaning. Meaning is nothing outside language; yet it is produced only by a systematic arrangement of differences in a structure or a system. This makes meaning an *effect* that cannot be detached from its material support. The meaning of an utterance or a text is not magically transferred from author to reader and can then be found *behind* the text or *between the lines* of what is said; meaning has to be *practically inscribed* on the surface of the opaque materiality that is written or spoken language. *Intended* meaning, as well as *objective* meaning, become concepts that are unworkable within the context of (post-)structuralist theory. Hermeneutics, born from the exegeses of biblical texts more than a millennium before the rise of structuralism, could still aspire to reach the distant horizon of the *original* meaning by applying rigorous methods of interpretation. Now, not meaning but the *production* of meaning could become the object of study.

If the signifier only relates to other signifiers and not to extra-linguistic entities in the material world, then *real* reference to anything outside language is impossible. There is no connection between the sign and its referent. Consequently, *reference* as such becomes a problem; language *refers* only to itself. In other words, the referent is *suspended* in a space that cannot be *symbolically represented* because it has its reality beyond the symbolic structure of differences within which only *internal* reference is possible. The world of referents becomes an unordered chaos that cannot be grasped without the mediation of language, which, however, does not reflect or represent reality, but lies parallel to it. That which is *outside* of language is, in Lacanian terms, 'the Real,' which 'resists symbolization absolutely' (Lacan 1991, p. 66).

This very general characterization of the diverse assemblage that is often designated as 'post-structuralism' at first glance seems to indicate a definite break from the Marxist theories discussed in the last chapter. The historicism of the materialist conception of history appears to be diametrically opposed to the *synchronic* way of studying social phenomena in semiological[10] approaches. The historical context, in the form of *diachronic* development or reference to the socio-historical situation of the phenomenon's emergence, is by and large excluded from structuralist inquiry. It only finds its way into analyses by means of references *internal* to the text (or utterance, or any other signifying practice). The impossibility of direct correspondence between external object and symbolic reference further obstructs (post-)structuralist engagement with history and unmediated material reality. Either history is conceived of as *text* (naturally without a referent) or it is something inaccessible bearing resemblance to Lacan's *Real*, mentioned above. Foucault, certainly influenced by structuralism in his earlier works, was a historian who surely did not think that history never happened, but his novel approach to his objects of study led more conservative historians as well as structuralist admirers alike to characterize him as 'an antihistorical historian' (Poster 1982, p. 116).

The problem of reference applies not only to history, but to present reality as well. There is no pre-linguistic reality that could be *expressed* in language. This is not to say that there is *no* reality and *only* language. More so, 'the entire field of *langue* lies parallel to reality itself' (Jameson 1974, p. 33). Describing economic structures, relations of production, etc., in short, what we have encountered as the *base* of a social formation is, even though there are *structures* and *relations* present, not immediately possible with a semiological/structuralist toolbox. Also, the fields of study are, at first glance, not the same as in Marxism. Language, signification, meaning are all elements of reality that were hardly considered central in early Marxist thinking. (Post-)structuralism mainly deals with 'superstructural' phenomena that, for better or for worse, are not theorized as *effects* of an extra-linguistic reality which determines them in some way or another.

It would be easy to list additional divergences from Marxist orthodoxy or present more Marxist criticisms of (post-)structuralism. Ridding theory of orthodoxies, like the Marxist and Freudian ones that were prevalent at that time, is one central characteristic of post-structuralism. But what seems of greater relevance to the present investigation is the fact that what is called 'post-structuralism' was and is heavily, if often ambivalently, influenced by Marxist theory.[11] In the present day, Žižek is probably the most prominent incarnation of the symbiosis of (post-structuralist) Lacanian psychoanalysis and Marxist thinking. Judith Butler was influenced by Marx as well as by Lukács and Althusser. Althusser himself—as well as his entire theory of structural Marxism—owes much to structuralist writers (such as Lévi-Strauss). Fredric Jameson, most definitely a Marxist, incorporates (post-)structuralist elements into his extensive writing on literature and culture. Deleuze and Guattari have very strong Marxist tendencies (cf. e.g. Jameson 1997) that are prominent in their defense of Marx in the first volume of *Capitalism and Schizophrenia* (Deleuze and Guattari 1983). And Lévi-Strauss writes in his *Savage Mind*: 'It is to this theory of superstructures, scarcely touched on by Marx, that I hope to make a contribution' (Lévi-Strauss 1966, p. 130). *Tel Quel*, a journal led by Sollers, was on the forefront in the development of deconstruction and post-structuralism and had Marxist affinities that expressed themselves first in their alliance with the French Communist Party and then in a flirtation with Maoism (on the journal, see Ffrench and Lack 1998, pp. 1ff.).

The Marxist understanding of history and its seeming incompatibility with (post-)structuralist theory remained an obstacle to overcome. Althusser dealt with that very problem and understood history—leaning on Lacan's *Real* and borrowing his vocabulary from Spinoza—as *absent cause*. Rather than implying that history is a text or a narrative with no *reality* outside its symbolic representation, Althusser's absent cause should be read as a concept of history that understands the latter as 'inaccessible to us except in textual form, and that our approach to it and to the Real itself necessarily passes through its prior textualization, its narrativization in the political unconscious' (Jameson 2002, p. 20).[12]

This relative inaccessibility of social reality and history has consequences for the conception of *material* conditions and the materiality of relations of production or that of modes of production. We will adjourn this problem and instead turn to another materiality.

THE MATERIALITY OF LANGUAGE

> *From the start the 'spirit' is afflicted with the curse of being 'burdened' with matter, which here makes its appearance in the form of agitated layers of air, sounds, in short, of language.*
> Karl Marx[13]

Language is a material phenomenon. It is material, because it consists of sounds—agitated air that sets matter in motion. In its textual form, language possesses a materiality that derives from markings—inscriptions—on pieces of paper, stone tablets, wooden planks, screens, a body, or any other surface. Gestures are material in their reliance on physical presence and bodily motion. These aspects of the materiality of language seem too obvious to have been missed in the millennia during which individuals have been thinking about language. Still, it was only a few decades ago that the implications of this materiality were systematically thought through and that language was analyzed and conceptualized as 'material,' albeit in a principally allusive way. The phonic, graphic, and gestural reality of language is not the only modality of materiality that has been ascribed to language. There is also the *opacity* of actualized signification which generates a resistance to immediate *understanding* and can be described as derivative of the primary materialities mentioned above—it also points at the fact that language is *not* composed of immaterial *ideas* that travel from one individual to another. Additionally, in structuralist and post-structuralist theories concerned with signification, the *facticity, effectivity,* and *lawfulness* of language is understood as a material dimension of signifying systems. Furthermore, language is understood as a material embodiment of varieties of social and political relations by some authors. To understand the ramifications of such an approach to language, the lines of argument involved will have to be briefly retraced.

That communication has a material *aspect* can hardly be denied.[14] Texts, utterances, and gestures depend on material support and so without a *medium* of some sort, inter-subjective, meaningful exchange is impossible. Disputes within theories of language oftentimes revolved around dichotomies that rested on the differentiation of material language and its immaterial counterpart, such as 'thought and language, spirit and matter, words and meaning, *langue* and *parole*, competence and performance, [and] mind and body' (Bleich 2013, p. 3). These binary oppositions, reminiscent of the dichotomies of the idealisms presented in Chap. 2, cannot easily be upheld in a materialist conception of language. To say that all language is material and thereby to suspend the search for an immaterial (mental or otherwise) essence of language that might be retrievable from behind or underneath the texts and utterances dissolves those binary oppositions. This assertion needs some explanation, as it is not immediately evident why *all* and *every* language is material.

We can begin by stressing that every system of signs has to be *processable* by others in order to be regarded as language. A *private* language that no one but its originator could understand is the definition of insanity—it would be reduced to the manic ramblings of a person unable to communicate. Semiology asserts that language has to be *exchanged* and that 'a language without speech would be impossible' (Barthes 1983, p. 26). So language must be understood in its dialogic reality (cf. e.g. Bachtin 1981,

p. 269). Because it is dialogic, it is dependent on its materialization. That is to say, for an utterance or a text to enter a (fictive) dialogue language has to be materialized. As Eagleton says about Bakhtin's theory, consciousness is the 'the subject's active, material, semiotic intercourse with others' (Eagleton 1996, p. 102).

That language is *material* intercourse with others is obvious in spoken language, where phonemes have to be strung together in order to *say something*. But phonemes cannot be connected randomly if a dialogic relation is to be established. They need to follow a code that is intersubjectively valid and knowable. Equally, written language is material and is required to be *readable* by at least one other person or be readable in the sense that its structure is *virtually* explicable. Hence it follows that language is fundamentally *social*. It is also fundamentally *material* because what is exchanged in 'communication' are sounds, inscriptions, gestures that reveal their social character in their iterability. Derrida, in *Signature Event Context*, writes:

> My communication must be repeatable—iterable—in the absolute absence of the receiver or of any empirically determinable collectivity of receivers. Such iterability... structures the mark of writing itself, no matter what particular type of writing is involved... A writing that is not structurally readable—iterable—beyond the death of the addressee would not be writing. (Derrida 1988, p. 7)

The potentiality of the absence of the receiver implies that the code be usable independently of the *presence* of the 'original' addressee. 'Usable' means repeatable in a context that is detached from both the presence of an author and of a determinable addressee. 'The possibility of repeating and thus of identifying the marks is implicit in every code, making it into a network... that is communicable, transmittable, decipherable, iterable for a third, and hence for every possible user in general' (Derrida 1988, p. 8). In the absence of the author the writing has to be materially present, otherwise—in the absence of the text that has already severed the connection to any presence of the author—there can be no iteration.

The *iterability* of the text hints at what reading accomplishes and simultaneously at what written language *transports*. Iteration—the repetition that never just repeats but shifts the meaning of what is iterated—qualifies the readability of the text. Not because it exposes the *literal* meaning of what is written but because it inserts the text into a structure of difference in which meaning can be produced. Then what is *communicated* in the writing? Simply the material markings, disjointed from the 'consciousness' and 'intention' of the writer-subject, devoid of literal meaning. This institutes a 'break with the horizon of communication as communication of consciousnesses or of presences and as linguistical or semantic transport of the desire to mean what one says' (Derrida 1988, p. 8).

The structure of difference that makes material signifiers iterable is a *material* 'network of regulated differences' which is realized 'by and in *concrete matter* and the *objective laws* of its organization' so that 'the actual body of language manifests a doubly discernible materiality' (Kristeva and Menke 1989, p. 18). For sounds and graphic signs to become *language*, 'regulated differences' are necessary. From the fact that there are laws it does not follow that a stable meaning can be attached to the markings of the text. These laws are conventions, rules—established in a social formation marked by dominance and inequality—that *materialize* in their actualization; they have no metaphysical validity outside their use. And what is more, rules are rules of use and are thus *contextually* and not universally applicable. What does this mark → [head] *mean* outside of a given context? Head of a procession, a state, a bridge, an animal? Simply something that is on top, in front of, the beginning of something?

With the last few paragraphs we have left behind the residual certitudes of Saussurean linguistics. For Saussure, *signifier* and *signified* are—arbitrarily connected as they may be—an indivisible unity in a relatively stable structure of differences. The *signifier*, which always relied on its material aspects to constitute the sound (or grapheme) image, now liberates itself *in its materiality* from the *signified*. It becomes matter waiting to be worked on within the restrictions set up by a network of differences—differences of *signifiers*, which don't gather around a master signifier with an original meaning attached to it that the others' meaning can be deduced from. To use Kittler's words, the 'materiality of signifiers rests on a chaos that defines them differentially' (Kittler 1990, p. 192). Within this chaos there is no Archimedean point from which the signifier could be lifted from its opacity.

With '*original*' meaning (the *origin* being the speaking or writing subject) banned from material language, and the concept of expression complicated by the fact that what is supposed to express (language) precedes what is meant to be expressed (ideas, feelings, perspectives), the relation between language and consciousness changes. Material, externalized language can no longer be thought of as an *instrument* of thought. The notion that it '*expresses*, as if it were a *tool*, something—an idea?—external to it' (Kristeva and Menke 1989, p. 7) cannot successfully be upheld. We are confronted, once again, with the idea as 'the other' of materiality. But what would such an idea be? Something that exists outside of and in another form than language? It seems impossible to assert the existence of ideas independent of a linguistic system without relapsing into idealism. We think *in language*. Its 'uttered, written or gestured materiality... produces and expresses (that is, communicates) what is known as thought,' and thus denies the *idea* its primacy because from this perspective 'language is at once the only manner of being of thought, its reality and its accomplishment' (ibid., p. 6). Thought is then a mute discourse which remains in the confines of the network of differences that is language.

In a materialist notion on language, speech thus forfeits its perceived authenticity. The *materiality of presence*, in the act of speaking, appears to fix the meaning of the materiality of the utterance. Gestures can point, underline and signal in order to restrict the excess of potential meaning of the utterance. Still, they too need to be *read* and understood. The signifying practice of gesturing obeys the rules of language. Gestures obtain meaning from their difference to all other gestures. The pointing finger *does* make a kind of reference possible, which the written text has no access to. One can say '*This* is the cat' and '*This* is the mat it sits on' and point at the two referents. In this way speech and gestures can refer to a shared environment—deictics ('I,' 'you,' 'here,' 'now') *function* much better.

It could be said, then, that language begins when the pointing no longer suffices, i.e. when the signification becomes *abstract*. From then on, the spoken word detaches itself from its source just like the text does. It was said that language is dialogical and directed at an *other*. In spoken language, the 'self' of the speaking subject becomes, in a sense, an 'other'—it is both addresser and addressee. The construction of *oneself as another* in language is an important process, which Paul Ricœur elaborated on extensively (e.g. Ricœur 1992, pp. 27ff.). Here, something more mundane than Ricœur's hermeneutics is meant: Each speaking subject addresses their utterance to themselves,

> since he[/she] is capable of emitting a message and deciphering it *at the same time*, and in principle does not emit anything he[/she] cannot decipher. In this way, the message intended for the *other* is, in a sense, *first* intended for the one who is speaking: whence it follows that to *speak* is to *speak to oneself*. (Kristeva and Menke 1989, p. 8)

Barthes provides an interesting insight that pertains to this facet of material speech. In *The Rustle of Language* (Barthes 1989b) he describes how the moment the utterance is materialized and has undergone the speaker's decipherment, it cannot be revised, nor taken back, except by *adding* more utterances. And paradoxically, this correcting by continuance is not necessitated by language's incapacity to convey meaning. A multiplicity of meaning lends itself to each utterance. 'Speech remains, it seems, condemned to stammering; writing, to silence and to the distinction of signs: in any case, there always remains *too much meaning* for language to fulfill a delectation appropriate to its substance' (ibid., p. 77). This delectation would be the rustle of language, comparable to the rustle of a working machine. The materiality of language permits no such rustle. Meaning and utterance do not coincide; and another utopia, where 'meaning, undivided, impenetrable, unnamable, would... be posited in the distance like a mirage, making the vocal exercise into a double landscape, phonemes being the "background" of our messages' with meaning as 'the vanishing point of our delectation' (ibid., p. 78) is improbable by the same token.

The *absence*, which we described as a condition for writing is also an element of speech. Speech is not pure *presence*; it gains a degree of independence from the speaker as soon as it is uttered. What Derrida calls *trace* (or almost interchangeably *différance*) denotes, among other things, the necessary *absence* of immediate *presence* in signification (cf. Derrida 1988, p. 50). As Kristeva writes in her introduction to Derrida's *Of Grammatology*, the nature of the sign is that 'half of it is always "not there" and the other half is always "not that." The structure of the sign is determined by the trace or track of that other which is forever absent' (Derrida 1976, p. xvii). If, consequently, from this perspective all language is a *trace*, then to be aware of signification is not to be aware of its immediate presence—it 'must already have happened; it is an event which is always in the past, even though in an immediate one' (Jameson 1974, p. 175). The fundamental absence of the speaking and writing subject in language forbids the understanding of speech and text as prolonged *presence*.

What will be shown in the following is how the *materiality of language* partakes in the decentering as well as the constitution of the subject. However, before we move on to the constitution of the subject in material language, we can assign the modalities of materiality encountered in our discussion to the categories developed in the investigation of Marxist materialism. There is, again, (1) the *positive materiality of matter* here consisting of sound waves, the bodies of gestures, and inscriptions on surfaces. These phonic, graphic, and gestural materials, however, become *language* only through *practices* of signification and meaning production, as this is what differentiates them from other sonic, visual, and haptic materialities. Therefore, (2) language possesses a *materiality of mutability* that refers to the fundamentally *processual* and *practical* character of language. Speaking, writing, gesturing, reading, understanding, etc. are *material practices* outside which language does not exist. Language, then, to recall Marx's critique of Feuerbach, should not be understood as an object of passive contemplation that confronts individuals in its materiality, but as a practical human activity that *materializes* in practices. Signifying practices depend on *codes* or 'regulated differences'—what Kristeva calls 'objective laws'—in order to function. (3) The *effectivity* and *facticity* of those laws exerts a material (i.e. *effective*) force on individuals, who must follow them if they want to communicate and interact. As we will see shortly, this *materiality of effectivity* can also be ascribed to the *institutions* that interpellate or otherwise subjectivate individuals (this is a notion that e.g. Coward and Ellis (e.g. 1977, p. 77), Foucault (e.g. 2002, p. 57), Leclercle (e.g. 2006, p. 166), and Pêcheux (e.g. 1982, pp. 110–111) share). The *positive materialities* just recalled can be subsumed under the *negative materiality* of language which designates its *real* existence and the fact that there are no such things as immaterial ideas or psychological states that exist independent from material language and could be thought *without* and expressed *in* language. Some of the implications of language's materiality for the concept of the subject found prominent expression in the discussions around the proclaimed 'Death of the Author,' to which we will turn now.

LANGUAGE AND THE AUTHOR-SUBJECT

The absence of the subject in material language means the end of the author. In the now seminal texts of Roland Barthes's *The Death of the Author* (Barthes 1989a), and Michel Foucault's reply in *What is an Author?* (Foucault 1998, pp. 205–224), the category of the writing subject, which expresses itself in literary language, was criticized from different perspectives. In both instances, the black-and-white materiality of the text removes the author-subject from the position of the origin of meaning.

In *The Death of the Author*, Barthes proclaims the absence of the writing subject from the written text and suggests to abandon the idea of a single, original meaning of literary works. In his text, two different kinds of argumentation can be identified. One line of argument could be described as *semiological*, the other as *hedonistic*. On the one hand, Barthes normatively calls for types of reading and writing that delimit the production of meaning by the reader (this productivity is the source of a kind of *jouissance*, hence the hedonistic quality of the argument). On the other hand, he argues (in proximity to Derrida) that the autonomy of the text results from the absence of the *scriptor* and the impossibility of decoding the play of differences among the material signifiers that constitute the text. Here, only the semiological implications, which are generalizable to material texts and are not limited to avant-garde literature, will be recounted.

For Barthes, 'writing is the destruction of every voice, every origin' (Barthes 1989a, p. 49). The author is absent in the practice of reading. At least, their potential absence—including the ultimate absence of death—is the condition for a writing that has as its addressee all those who can read (or will be able to in the future). The absence of the writing individual not only prohibits the use of ostensive deixis that is possible in situated discourses of mutual presence; it also dissolves the possibility of reference to a shared environment. As soon as writing is released from its situational, *performative* obligation—a writing that does not act on its immediate surroundings—a 'gap appears, the voice loses its origin, the author enters into his own death, writing begins' (ibid.).

What weighs more heavily, however, is that the text's *materiality* introduces an opacity, which makes its deciphering a futile task. The material signifiers that make up the inscriptions on the surface of the document are actualized *langue* (cf. Barthes 1983, p. 47). Their meaning is not directly accessible or evident. They are, initially, the material (signifying) side of the sign, which depends on the signified to be complete. Now, the signified of the text is absent and the mass of signifiers awaits its *disentanglement* by the reader. But what the author *intended* the text to mean cannot be reconstructed. The text is not the Marathonian messenger, whose way was *one* with his message. The text emancipates itself from the author at the moment it is written. Its *materiality* sets up a boundary that does not permit the immediate transmission of intended meaning, local reference, expressed inner states, in short, it does not allow access to the author as origin of meaning.

A text's structure can be followed but the text itself cannot be definitively deciphered. The text consists not of a line of words, releasing a single 'theological' meaning (the 'message' of the Author-God), but of a multi-dimensional space in which are married and contested several writings, none of which is original: the text is a fabric of quotations, resulting from a thousand sources of culture. (Barthes 1989a, pp. 52–53)

The multiplicity of writings is due to the phenomenon Kristeva would later call *intertextuality* (cf. Kristeva 1980, pp. 36ff.). It points to the fact that the meaning of a (literary) text is not transferred from author to reader but *mediated doubly* by the materiality of the text and by structures of meaning-production derived from other texts. Simultaneously it indicates the author's (and reader's) involvement in *language* and literature, both of which precede them.

In literature, a 'mode of writing is pre-eminently social, it is a use of language which pre-dates the writer and forms the writer like language itself: it is a sociolect' (Coward and Ellis 1977, p. 38). *How* the author writes never simply *expresses* their innermost self. Their *self*, the interior 'thing' that could be *translated* into language 'is itself no more than a ready-made lexicon, whose words can be explained only through other words, and this ad infinitum' (Barthes 1989a, p. 53). Thus the author dies two deaths: from the moment of writing they are absent from the text, lose control over it, and the connection between author and text is severed; and also, they were never a centered subject expressing themselves in the first place. It is always 'language which speaks, not the author' (Barthes 1989a, p. 50). The text consists not of *ideas* or *thoughts*, but of *signifiers* that are material.

Paul Ricoeur has a similar approach to texts. For him, the references of the text are internal, and original meaning can never be determined (the 'text frees its meaning from the tutelage of the mental intention, it frees its reference from the limits of ostensive reference' Ricœur 1973, p. 96). At the same time there is a 'spirituality of writing,' which is 'the counterpart of its materiality' (ibid., p. 97). In the *interpretation* by the reader, the reference of the text escapes the confines of its internal referentiality and can be made to refer to the life-world of the reader. In Barthes's approach, such reference seems impossible. For him, what gives the text a meaning is not the message the author sent, but the one the reader produces. The text refers to itself, and the reader creatively *produces* its meaning, albeit in the limits set by the structure of language and the signifying systems of literature.

Michel Foucault shares with Barthes the critique of an understanding of writing as the expression of subjectivity. Like Barthes, he sees texts as 'an interplay of signs arranged less according to its signified content than according to the very nature of the signifier' (Foucault 1998, p. 206). Barthes presented the concept of the author as an instance that limits the text by seeking the *one* original meaning. The assumption that there *was* such a meaning inhibited the *writable* text that the reader creatively produced in their reading. Similarly, Foucault describes the author (as a *function*) as 'the ideological figure by which one marks the manner in which we fear the proliferation of meaning' (Foucault 1998, p. 222). Explaining the literary work in recourse to the author's life and psychology imposes a false coherence on it. Foucault, rather than *determining* who speaks in a text, wants to reach a point where the question is: 'what does it matter who speaks?' For him, the more pertinent questions are:

> How, under what conditions, and in what forms can something like a subject appear in the order of discourse? What place can it occupy in each type of discourse, what functions can it assume, and by obeying what rules? In short, it is a matter of depriving the subject (or its substitute) of its role as originator, and of analyzing the subject as a variable and complex function of discourse. (Foucault 1998, p. 221)

Instead of a void, there is now a subject that can be analyzed as a *function of discourse*. The roles attributed to subject and discourse in classical literary criticism and theory are hereby reversed. A text is not 'determined by' or 'a result of' the writing subject and its biography and psychology; the subject itself is a *function* of discourse (a function, which does not disappear by proclaiming the death of the author).

The author, as understood by Barthes, could only disappear from the text by effacing 'the more visible marks of the author's empiricity' (Foucault 1998, p. 208). As we will see shortly, there are signs, hints, and instructions (like *shifters*) in the text that can be explicated and analyzed to reveal *subject positions* opened up by the text, while we never arrive at the author's expressions or intentions. This is not, however, a return to the concept of an author-subject, which Barthes criticized. Foucault returns to the question of the subject not 'in order to reestablish the theme of an originating subject but to grasp the subject's points of insertion, modes of functioning, and system of dependencies' (Foucault 1998, pp. 209–210).

In Barthes as well as Foucault, the author as origin of meaning sustains heavy blows. It can no longer be conceived of as the fixed point from which meaning emanates. An excess of possible meaning(s) is present in every text that cannot be *satisfyingly* reduced by evoking an author-subject. Conventional criticism—the approach to literature criticized by Barthes and Foucault alike—attempts a closure of this troubling plurality of meaning; it 'aims at an interpretation, fixing a meaning, finding a source (the author) and an ending, a closure (the meaning)' (Coward and Ellis 1977, p. 45). Where does the discrediting of such criticism leave us in regard to *the subject in material language?*[16]

It would appear we have reached a juncture that offers two paths: Either we watch the subject die (it is, in any case, not the fount of meaning, the center of experience, or the autonomous point that refers back to itself) or we turn to its constitution and functioning in language and discourse without falling behind what we have learned so far. Several approaches within 'post-structuralism' or in its direct vicinity retrace or theorize the emergence—albeit decentered and split—of a subject in language or discourse.

THE CONSTITUTION OF THE SUBJECT IN MATERIAL DISCOURSE

What we have seen so far is that language and discourse are material and that the definitive meaning neither of an utterance nor of a text can be determined. We have further established that the subject does not precede language and is not the center from which meaning flows. The fact that it is only through language that we communicate with others and experience the world, that, in fact, there is no thought outside language, further destabilized the concept of an autonomous, self-conscious subject. Furthermore, the social character of every language, its dependence on *the other*, makes a private language, in which an imaginary subject could genuinely think and feel, impossible.

Still, we experience each other as subjects and mostly *know* what a word or sentences means. We also feel like we are the source of our thoughts and experiences. The obviousness with which language and meaning are experienced opens up the question of what kind of subject is produced as well as necessitated by language. Approaches that see the subject as constructed in language (through discourse or ideology) have in common the critique of the Cartesian *Cogito* and the understanding of the subject as *contingent* and not deductible from a human essence. The remainder of this chapter will deal with some such approaches and present the mechanism by and through which subjects are constituted in relation to the material instances of discourse and the social as *ideological and discursive subject positioning practices.*

The dialogical and social nature of language cannot be reduced to a model of communication in which a sender transmits a message to a receiver, who then deciphers it correctly. Such a conception obscures the way 'in which language sets up the positions of *I* and *you* that are necessary for communication to take place at all' (Coward and Ellis 1977, p. 79). We already mentioned that the speaker is at the same time the destinee of their message, capable of deciphering it. Thus the utterance was detached from the speaking subject. Deictic markers such as *I* leave *traces* of the production situation (the enunciation) of an utterance, but at this very basic level utterances could be said to always be *shifted out*,[17] away from the speaking subject. So already here, the *I* of the utterance is not identical with the speaking subject. Yet, the positions of the *I* and *you* that are necessary for language use are equally important in the construction of subjectivity through language.

From a Lacanian point of view, each linguistic situation presupposes a kind of subject in that it involves, as Jameson notes in *The Prison-House of Language,*

> not only an abstract category of otherness that precedes all empirical experi-
> ence of the other, not only a concrete and empirical other person also, but,
> together with those two elements, yet a third, which is my own alter-ego, or
> my image of myself. (Jameson 1974, p. 171)

The subject in language, then, appears to be always-already there as the entity that has an image of itself. Kristeva, in the same vein, writes that 'language is possible only because each speaker sets himself up as a *subject* by referring to himself as *I* in the discourse' (Kristeva and Menke 1989, p. 35).

The question remains who that thing is that is set up and/or sets itself up as a *subject*. And furthermore, if language is antecedent to the subject, then how can the latter be the condition of the former? Preliminarily, it can be said that there is no subject before language and that there is no language without a speaker who can say *I*. Benveniste put it nicely when he wrote that 'subjectivity' 'is the capacity of the speaker to posit himself as "subject"' and it is only 'the emergence in the being of a fundamental property of language. "Ego" is he who says "ego." That is where we see the foundation of "subjectivity"' (Benveniste 1973, p. 224).[18] Again, it looks like the speaker capable of positing themself as a subject already *is* a subject, while its emergence is a *function* of language. To simply claim that the subject is constructed by language and that language *necessitates* certain subjects is, however, not enough.[19] It would mean positing a kind of effectivity and determination *by and through language* that resembles what Althusser denounced as 'expressive causality.' Discourse and language thus present themselves as an entity that acts on elements in a social formation while being *independent* from the utterances and enunciations that constitute it. If language does not produce subjects by *expressing* itself in speaking and writing subjects, there must be another mechanism at work that *enables* individuals to say *I* and thus enter language. It should be clear by now that putting the subject back in the center by asserting that it creates itself by its *capacity* to posit itself as subject and saying *I* would be just as regressive as maintaining, idealistically, that it is language (and nothing else) that imprints itself on blank individuals, converting them to subjects in and of the prison-house of language.

To construe the matter dialectically by holding that 'it could be argued that not only do human beings use language to reproduce themselves, multiply their power and knowledge, etcetera, but also… language itself uses human beings to replicate and expand itself, to gain new wealth of meanings, etcetera' (Žižek 1998, p. 254) is not false—but it does not tell us *how* language uses and produces subjects. Returning to the concept of ideology and in a next step conceptualizing *subject positions* that are provided in a social formation can help understand how the *positionality* of the speaking and writing subject constitutes it and enables it to produce meaning.

Language and Ideology: The Subject Interpellated by Discourse

The connection between theories of language and concepts of ideology was made long before the *linguistic turn*. The Russian linguist and Marxist Valentin Vološinov wrote his highly influential book[20] *Marxism and the Philosophy of Language* in 1929. In it, he asserts that everything 'ideological possesses *meaning*: it represents, depicts, or stands for something lying outside itself. In other words, it is a *sign*. *Without signs, there is no ideology*' (Vološinov 1973, p. 9). Further, he writes that signs only emerge in social *interaction* with others. Because what is called 'consciousness' is 'filled with signs' it only *becomes* consciousness 'once it has been filled with ideological (semiotic) content, consequently, only in the process of social interaction' (ibid., p. 11). Not only did Vološinov anticipate the *signifying* and *social* dimension of ideology, he recognized also the *material* character of ideology in language. Each *ideological sign* is, for him, not simply a

> reflection, a shadow, of reality, but is also itself a *material* segment of that very reality. Every phenomenon functioning as an ideological sign has some kind of *material embodiment*, whether in sound, physical mass, color, movements of the body, or the like. (Ibid.)

It should be noted, if only in passing, that some scholars believe the true author of *Marxism and the Philosophy of Language* was Bakhtin, with whom Vološinov shared a friendship and the interest in linguistics.[21] The undeniable similarity of their theories is apparent, for instance, in Eagleton's characterization of Bakhtin's philosophy. He writes that for Bakhtin,

> all signs were material—quite as material as bodies or automobiles—and since there could be no human consciousness without them, Bakhtin's theory of language laid the foundation for a materialist theory of consciousness itself in which language was not to be seen either as 'expression,' 'reflection' or abstract system, but rather as a material means of production, whereby the material body of the sign was transformed through a process of social conflict and dialogue into meaning. (Eagleton 1996, p. 102)

While Bakhtin and Vološinov developed linguistic theories that gave a materialist account of the relationship between material language, ideology, and consciousness, it was Michel Pêcheux, who, taking his departure from structural linguistics and Althusser's theory of ideology, set out to develop a materialist theory of discourse that links 'the question of the *constitution of meaning* to that of the *constitution of the subject*' while understanding this linking as 'located inside the "central thesis" itself, in the figure of *interpellation*' (Pêcheux 1982, pp. 104–105). In this perspective, meaning and the subject are produced according to *subject-positions* in discursive formations.

In Althusser, ideology interpellates individuals into subject-positions from which they enter *symbolic* relations with other subjects and their conditions of existence. The relation between the *Logos* of ideology and that of language was already mentioned. We are now in a position to say that the *representations* of the imaginary relationships of individuals to their real material conditions of existence cannot take place outside of language and discourse. Ideological subjects can be conceived of as constructed *for* these representations and as an effect of discursive practices. There is no discourse without subject and thus every 'discourse has, as its necessary correlate, a subject, which is one of the effects, if not the major effect, of its functioning. Ideological discourse "produces" or "induces" a subject-effect, a subject' (Althusser 2014, p. 85).

The symbolic position ideology provides is the very basis of the subject's activity and is the condition of its *positioning* as a coherent whole. Ideology, then, 'produces the subject as the place where a specific meaning is realized in signification' (Coward and Ellis 1977, p. 68). Subjects do not only *practically* represent an imaginary relation to their conditions of existence, they *live* their imaginary relationship as a *meaningful* one. However, as we have seen, meaning cannot be produced outside signification, which implies that a theory of ideology necessitates a theory of the relation of subjects to signification. Althusser, as we saw earlier, was evidently influenced by Lacan's concept of the Symbolic Order,[22] which refers to

> that realm into which the child emerges, out of a biological namelessness, when he gradually acquires language. It is impersonal, or superpersonal, but it is also that which permits the very sense of identity itself to come into being. Consciousness, personality, the subject are, therefore... secondary phenomena which are determined by the vaster structure of language itself, or of the Symbolic. (Jameson 1974, c.1972, p. 130)

The capacity of saying *I*, the possibility of symbolic representation, and the material *practices* that ideology depends on take place in a symbolic order that puts the individual in the position of a homogeneous subject in relation to meaning. The *material actions inserted into material practices* that Althusser writes about must, consequently, be understood as *material signifying practices*, or, better, as *material discursive positioning practices*.

In Pêcheux's discourse theory individuals are *interpellated-identified* 'as speaking-subjects (as subjects of *their* discourse) by the discursive formations which represent "in language" the ideological formations that correspond to them' (Pêcheux 1982, p. 112). What is added to Althusser's notion of ideology is, thus, the qualification of the interpellated individuals as *speaking* subjects in *discursive formations*,[23] in which they take up a subject-position that exists *anterior to* the individual entering discourse. Althusser, in *Ideology and Ideological State Apparatuses*, purports that 'the category of the subject is a primary "obviousness" [and like] all obviousnesses, including those that make a word "name a thing" or "have a meaning"… the obviousness that you and I are subjects… is an ideological effect, the elementary ideological effect' (Althusser 1972, pp. 171–172). And he adds, in a footnote, that *linguists* 'run up against difficulties which arise because they ignore the action of the ideological effects in all discourses' (ibid, p. 172, n. 16). Pêcheux further develops this side note, arguing that the 'evidentness' of *meaning* cannot be separated from the 'evidentness' of the subject's identity.

That we are subjects and that what we hear and say, read and write has meaning (and which meaning that is) is evident to us—just as evident as our relationships to our conditions of existence. There is no need to dwell again on the fact that words don't have meaning in themselves. The consequence, however, that Pêcheux draws from his observations that in the face of this fact meaning is still an *evidentness* deserves our attention. He claims that '*words, expressions, propositions, etc., change their meaning according to the positions held by those who use them,*' which means that those meanings are produced 'by reference to those positions, i.e., by reference to the ideological formations… in which those positions are inscribed' (Pêcheux 1982, p. 111). Thereby, meaning becomes an ideological effect tied to the individual's interpellation as a subject into a *discursive* subject-position. What is more, understanding meaning as dependent on subject-positions allows us to understand what Pêcheux calls *the material character of the meaning*, obscured by the 'evidentness' afforded by the apparent 'transparency of language.' Words find their meaning in accordance with positions within *material discursive formations* that are inextricably linked to ideological practice and the respective *material* conditions from which discursive formations arise.

The symbolic position from which the subject represents the imaginary relationship to their conditions of existence cannot be occupied without this 'evidentness' of meaning which allows for the production of unquestioned 'truths' (*I am I*, etc.). Revising Althusser, Pêcheux maintains that the operation of Ideology in general as the interpellation of individuals as subjects (and specifically as subjects for their discourse) is realized through the complex of ideological formations... and supplies 'each subject' with his 'reality' as a system of evident truths and significations perceived-accepted-suffered. (Ibid., p. 113)

Thus, individuals are interpellated *through* language as speaking subjects who can *live* their (meaningful) imaginary relationship to their real material conditions of existence.

The Subject as Position

The concept of subject-positions we have availed ourselves of above can be approached from different angles. In regard to the speaking subject, subject-positions are necessary to *fix* meaning and put the subject in relation to other subjects and the discursive/ideological/social formation(s) they inhabit. A *meaningful* relation to the subject's reality is possible only from a certain, definite position occupied by the subject in relation to language. Using Saussurean vocabulary, it can be recalled that signifier and signified are not only connected arbitrarily but that their connection is not stable and has to be produced. The production of meaning thus entails the *attaching* of signifiers to signifieds, which—as we have seen—can never produce definitive meaning. Coward and Ellis suggest that the relation of signifier and signified 'becomes fixed when the conscious subject is constructed in a certain position in relation to the signifying chain' (Coward and Ellis 1977, p. 8). Subject-positions *provide* a space from which subjects can say *I* and from which they can produce meaning. They are what gives the subject an identity and enables them to speak. Again, the positioning of the subject is a process that takes place in language, or *discourse*.

For Pêcheux as well as Foucault *discursive* formations create subject positions that can—and must—be occupied by speaking individuals. To be a subject is always to occupy a space from which one speaks.[24] I speak *as* a daughter, a communist, a doctor, a boy, etc. and in discourse I am addressed as such. The concept of subject-positions should not be identified with a social *role* or an *identity*, though. They are, first and foremost, *discursive* and *symbolic* positions tied to the use of *material* language, in the sense introduced above. The process by which an individual is *subjectified* in discourse is, in this approach, 'understood as the appropriation of a subject position which had already been defined anterior to the individual's entry into discourse' (Angermuller 2009, p. 113).

By occupying a definite subject-position, the subject is enabled to experience itself as a unified whole ('of course I am me and no other!') and *speak* and *act* as a subject. From this it by no means follows that the speaking and writing subject *really is* a unified whole. The unity is a linguistic illusion afforded by the use of language. And we can add that, unsurprisingly, not even in this *use of language* does the subject present itself as the uniform entity that speaks with *one* voice producing *one* meaning—the subject is split.

Arguing for a *split* subject, which is dispersed in material language, entails abandoning the search for the subject behind what is said and written. From the subject-oriented perspective taken so far, the setting up and occupying of subject-positions can be described as processes in which the ideological subject is constituted. In this process, the subject is *present* and '*in person* forms part of ideological discourse… since it is itself a determinate signifier of this discourse' (Althusser 2014, p. 85). Shifting the position to a reader-oriented perspective can, without contradicting what was just said, make visible the operations by which subject-positions are *assigned* in discourse. We will close this chapter with the presentation of some aspects of an enunciative-pragmatic approach to discourse. This will give us a better idea of the functioning of (ideological) subject positioning practices.

In spoken language and texts, including those produced by a *single* author or speaker, multiple subject-positions can be identified—none of which can easily be assigned to the subject producing the linguistic material. Stating this is not the same as repeating that a text or an utterance has various possible *meanings*. It is partly *because* of 'the opaque materiality' of texts that 'meaning cannot be read from the surface' (Angermuller 2014, p. 3) and has to be produced. Similarly, the opacity of material language prevents the text from being assignable to a single speaking/writing subject. Not only are different subject-positions present in an utterance (many of them opposing and contradicting each other), but also the subjects in discourse *occupy* different subject-positions, which cannot be conceptualized as being generated from a stable center. The positions opened up by and occupied in the text or utterance can be analyzed and made explicit. Foucault, for example, states that enunciations[25] always have some relation to *a* subject. This enunciative subject, however, is not identical with the empirical individual appropriating a subject-position in a discursive formation and then writes or speaks from that position. Neither is it the grammatical subject that can be found in the sentences of the utterance. Rather, he argues that 'the subject is an "empty function". It is a particular structure of a locus which individuals can occupy. Statements imply or require particular subject positions to be occupied' (Cousins and Hussain 1984, p. 92).

Earlier, we quoted Foucault as saying that there are 'more visible marks of the author's empiricity.' We can now shortly mention two aspects of approaches concerned with the *polyphony* of (primarily textual) discourse—the many *voices* discernible in texts—both of which concern the subject. In this context, discourse can be understood as 'a linguistically encoded practice of positioning oneself and others and creating discursive relationships with others within a play of polyphonic voices' (Angermuller 2014, p. 4). On the one hand, such approaches do not foreclose the *situation* in which an utterance emerged (i.e. they reintroduce the *context* that structural approaches had excluded from their analyses), but find the traces of the enunciation *in the text*. On the other hand, they analyze the different subject-positions opened up by the text, none of which coincide with the empirical 'psychological' entity of the subject producing the enunciation.

In its materiality a text does not allow the determination of its definitive situation of production. Neither can the situational context (*énonciation*) in which the text was written be reconstructed exactly, nor can the *producer* of the text be ascertained in a way that would allow a minute description of intentions, precise meanings, or the inner workings of their *subjectivity*. It is possible, however, to find *traces*, or *markers* of the enunciation in the text and reconstruct the *context* that the text itself mobilizes and produces simultaneously. Above, we mentioned that utterances are *shifted out*, away from their production situation.[26] The converse operation, *shifting in*, moves the utterance toward the enunciation. Markers of such an operation are, for example deictics like *I*, *here*, *now* that provide a context of enunciation by positioning the *locutor*[27] spatially and temporally (cf. e.g. Greimas and Courtés 1982, pp. 87ff). The locutor, however, who belongs 'to the utterance and cannot be anchored in a speaking subject or in *one* individual out there in the world' (Angermuller 2009, p. 122) gives us no access to anything related to the author-subject that both Foucault and Barthes reject. At the same time, formal instructions—like the aforementioned deictics—that the text gives the reader make it possible to produce *a* meaning of the material and position it in a specific discourse.

The content of what is written, then, not only is 'deciphered' but can be attributed to various subject-positions. At this point, it suffices to say that the different contents or meanings can be assigned to 'the author (or locutor) and the Other(s) (allocutor or addressee) of discourse' (Angermuller 2012, p. 120), among others. The different positions from which the text or utterance is spoken constitute its *polyphony*. There are many voices present that are in a dialogue *with each other*. Markers of such polyphony are, for instance, *not*s and *but*s which construct a subject position within the text that is rejected by the locutor. In a nutshell, a sentence like 'The sun is *not* more than 200 years old' manifests a position that says 'The sun is more than 200 years old' of which the first sentence is the negation. Similarly, a newspaper article that states 'In this time of unprecedented crisis, Germany should *not* shoot refugee children trying to cross the border' implicates a position from which is said 'In this time of unprecedented crisis, Germany should shoot refugee children trying to cross the border.'[28]

If these formal instructions in the form of markers of indexicality and polyphony were said to enable the reader to produce meaning, we can now add that they enable a contextualization of the text, in which the reader connects the subject-positions discernible in the material to extra-textual individuals. *Understanding* the newspaper article depends, among many other things, on being able to identify who occupies the subject-position from which is said 'Germany should shoot refugee children.' But does that mean that the reader *finds* the context that existed before the text and *correctly identifies* the occupants of the positions traceable? No. Rather, the text and context should be seen as mutually determining. The text produces its own context and mobilizes subject-positions. This complex play of producing, assigning and occupying subject-positions is part of the process of the subject's subjectivation by and in language. By analyzing the different subject-positions mobilized in predominantly text-based discourse, an enunciative-pragmatic approach offers a 'poststructuralist discourse analysis' (Angermuller 2014), which 'accounts for the construction of subjectivity in the many voices of discourse' while maintaining a 'preference for the non-subjectivist study of discursive subjectivity' (ibid. pp. 2–3).

Concluding this part of our survey, we can sum up by saying that the subject is an effect of social processes and practices that could be shown to be constituted as well as decentered in material discursive practices. The materiality of language was presented as irreducible to simply matter or matter in motion. Rather, it was evidenced that the manifold ways in which discourse and language are material rest on the interrelated modalities of *positive*, *processual*, and *effective* materiality developed in earlier chapters. Altogether we have not strayed too far from the Marxist-materialist framework set up in Chapters 3 and 4. In many ways, the engagement with (post-)structuralist theory enriched and refined some of the concepts encountered in the discussion of Marxist materialism. Thus, for instance, our understanding of the mechanism of ideology could be sharpened and the role of material language in the constitution of the subject was brought to the fore.

The authors we will engage with now are of a different ilk than those dealt with so far. They could be said to harbor a certain 'hostility to Marxist materialism' (Noys 2015, p. 1) and oftentimes their approach is presented as being in a dangerous vicinity to the theories of New Materialism with their '"thing-power" materialism' (Bennett 2010a, p. 47) and enchanted *vibrant matter* (Bennett 2010b). Nevertheless, there are very good reasons to include the approaches of *material semiotics* in our investigation. They conceptualize materiality in a non-reductionist way and provide a novel perspective on the subject and its relation to the material. Furthermore, the reading of this group of texts, which are presented below, will emphasize aspects of materiality and subjectivity omitted thus far.

NOTES

1. The content of the book can be summed up in one quote: 'QUESTION: Is it true that language is a superstructure on a base? ANSWER: No, it is not true' (Stalin 1972, p. 3).
2. But see, for example de Freitas and Curinga (2015).
3. See, for example the contributions by Balibar, Derrida, Nancy, Deleuze, Irigaray, and Rancière in the book *Who Comes After the Subject?* (Cadava *et al.* 1991).
4. The book was compiled from notes by some of Saussure's students in Switzerland.
5. Cf. e.g. the introduction to Angermuller's book with the telling title Why *There Is No Poststructuralism in France* (Angermuller 2015, pp. 1ff, or Angermuller 2009, pp. 15f.). Both books also give very useful accounts of the intellectual movement of 'post-structuralism'.
6. The term was coined by Richard Rorty's book *The Linguistic Turn* (Rorty 1992).
7. See, for instance, his article 'Language and the Analysis of Social Laws' (Lévi-Strauss 1951).
8. Cf. e.g. Bowie 2010, p. 37.
9. Here too, Nietzsche, who would become a major reference for 'post-structuralists' like Deleuze or Foucault preempted those ideas. In his early notebooks, he describes the impossibility to think outside the constraints of

language and notes: 'Language, the word, nothing but symbol. Thinking, i.e. consciously imagining, is nothing but envisioning and linking linguistic symbols' (Nietzsche 2009, p. 27).

10. 'Semiology' and 'semiological' is here used to designate the Saussurean notion of semiotics. In the subsequent chapter (Chapter 6), semiotics will be used to designate the study of signs and meaning.

11. Jameson writes that 'they know Marx so well as to seem constantly on the point of translating him into something else' (Jameson 1974, p. 102).

12. Althusser does not speak of the political unconscious. That aspect in the characterization of Althusser's understanding of history was added by the great Fredric Jameson.

13. Marx and Engels (1965, pp. 41–42).

14. At least not since Marshall McLuhan's famous chapter titled 'The Medium is the Message' in 'Understanding Media: The Extensions of Man' (McLuhan 1994, pp. 7ff).

15. For an interesting approach to this problem, see Michaels (2004, especially pp. 11ff.).

16. Shifting out or disengagement are defined by Greimas and Courtés as 'the operation by which the domain of the enunciation disjuncts and projects forth from itself, at the moment of the language act and in view of manifestation, certain terms bound to its base structure, so as thereby to constitute the foundational elements of the discourse-utterance' (Greimas and Courtés 1982, p. 87). And Bruno Latour remarks rightly that 'nothing can be said of the enunciator of a narration if not in a narration where the enunciator becomes a shifted-out character' (Latour 1988, p. 27).

17. From a slightly different perspective, Regenia Gagnier, who understands subjectivity and the subject as a mode of self-representation in language, writes: 'First, the subject is a subject to itself, an "I," however difficult or even impossible it may be for others to understand this "I" from its own viewpoint, within its own experience' (Gagnier 1991, p. 8).

18. And it is not what Benveniste does. But the quote illustrates a point, namely, that it is hard to find an entry point into the process of subjectivation by language.

19. The book influenced, for example, Roman Jakobson (cf. especially the chapter 'Shifters and Verbal Categories' in Jakobson 1990, pp. 386ff.).

20. On this theory, see: Clark and Holquist (1984).

21. The difference to Lacan's Symbolic Order is that Althusser sees the individual subjected before language acquisition.

22. He defines a discursive formation as that which 'in a given ideological formation [of ISAs], i.e., from a given position in a given conjuncture determined by the state of the class struggle, determines what can and should be said' (Pêcheux 1982, p. 111).

23. The position in the discursive formation also determines what can and should be said. For example, it makes a difference from which subject-position I diagnose someone with a disease (doctor, veterinarian, philosopher...).
24. Enunciation can here be understood as the production situation of the text or utterance.
25. Literature makes wide use of this operation to convey a sense of realism. When Boris Pasternak writes in *Doctor Zhivago*: 'One evening at the end of November Yuri came home late from the university; he was tired and had eaten nothing all day' (Pasternak 1959, p. 69), the reader (enunciatee) is lead away from Pasternak at his study in Moscow. Instead, the reader's attention is moved to an actor (Yuri), at another time (one evening at the end of November in the last century), in another place (Yuri's home). There is actantial disengagement, which consists of a disjunction of a 'not-I' from the subject of the enunciation, and projection into the utterance; temporal disengagement, which postulates a 'not-now' distinct from the time of the enunciation; and spatial disengagement, which opposes a 'not-here' to the place of the enunciation (cf. Greimas and Courtés 1982, p. 88).
26. Who is 'the deictic center of the enunciation' (Angermuller 2009, p. 122).
27. That there is 'an unprecedented time of crisis' functions as a preconstructed that does not have to be explained anymore and is presented as common knowledge. The concept of the preconstructed goes back to Pêcheux (cf. e.g. Pêcheux 1982, p. 64).

REFERENCES

Althusser, L. (1972). Ideology and ideological state apparatuses (notes towards an investigation). In L. Althusser (Ed.), *Lenin and philosophy, and other essays* (pp. 127–188). New York: Monthly Review Press.

Althusser, L. (2014). Three notes on the theory of discourses. In J. Angermuller, D. Maingueneau, & R. Wodak (Eds.), *The discourse studies reader: Main currents in theory and analysis* (pp. 83–88). Amsterdam: John Benjamins Publishing.

Angermuller, J. (2009). After structuralism: The discourse of theory and the intellectual field in France. Unpublished Manuscript.

Angermuller, J. (2012). Fixing meaning: The many voices of the post-liberal hegemony in Russia. *JLP, 11*(1), 115–134.

Angermuller, J. (2014). *Poststructuralist discourse analysis: Subjectivity in enunciative pragmatics*. Basingstoke: Palgrave Macmillan.

Angermuller, J. (2015). *Why there is no poststructuralism in France: The making of an intellectual generation*. London: Bloomsbury Academic.

Austin, J. L. (1962). *How to do things with words.* Oxford: Clarendon Press.

Bachtin, M. M. (1981). *The dialogic imagination: Four essays.* Austin, TX: University of Texas Press.

Barthes, R. (1972). *Mythologies.* New York: Noonday Press.

Barthes, R. (1983). *Elements of semiology.* New York: Hill & Wang.

Barthes, R. (1989a). The death of the author. In R. Barthes (Ed.), *The rustle of language* (pp. 49–55). Berkeley: University of California Press.

Barthes, R. (1989b). The rustle of language. In R. Barthes (Ed.), *The rustle of language* (pp. 76–79). Berkeley: University of California Press.

Bennett, J. (2010a). A vitalist stopover on the way to a new materialism. In D. H. Coole & S. Frost (Eds.), *New materialisms: Ontology, agency, and politics* (pp. 47–69). Durham, NC: Duke University Press.

Bennett, J. (2010b). *Vibrant matter: A political ecology of things.* Durham: Duke University Press.

Benveniste, E. (1973). *Problems in general linguistics.* Florida: University of Miami Press.

Bleich, D. (2013). *The materiality of language: Gender, politics, and the university.* Bloomington: Indiana University Press.

Bowie, A. (2010). *German philosophy: A very short introduction.* Oxford: Oxford University Press.

Cadava, E., Connor, P., & Nancy, J.-L. (Eds.). (1991). *Who comes after the subject?* New York: Routledge.

Clark, K., & Holquist, M. (1984). *Mikhail Bakhtin.* Cambridge, MA: Harvard University Press.

Cousins, M., & Hussain, A. (1984). *Michel Foucault.* London: Macmillan.

Coward, R., & Ellis, J. (1977). *Language and materialism: Developments in semiology and the theory of the subject.* London, Boston: Routledge & Paul.

de Freitas, E., & Curinga, M. X. (2015). New materialist approaches to the study of language and identity: Assembling the posthuman subject. *Curriculum Inquiry, 45*(3), 249–265.

de Saussure, F. (1986). *Course in general linguistics.* LaSalle, IL: Open Court.

Deleuze, G., & Guattari, F. (1983). *Anti-Oedipus: Capitalism and schizophrenia.* Minneapolis: University of Minnesota Press.

Derrida, J. (1976). *Of grammatology.* Baltimore: Johns Hopkins University Press.

Derrida, J. (1988). *Limited Inc.* Evanston, IL: Northwestern University Press.

Duranti, A. (1997). *Linguistic anthropology.* New York: Cambridge University Press.

Eagleton, T. (1996). *Literary theory: An introduction.* Minneapolis, MN: University of Minnesota Press.

Edwards, J. (2009). *Language and identity: An Introduction.* Cambridge: Cambridge University Press.

Ffrench, P., & Lack, R.-F. (1998). *The tel quel reader.* London: Routledge.

Foucault, M. (1998). *Aesthetics, method and epistemology (Essential works, 1954–1984, Vol. 2)*. New York: New Press.

Foucault, M. (2002). *The order of things: An archaeology of the human sciences*. London: Routledge.

Gagnier, R. (1991). *Subjectivities: A history of self-representation in Britain, 1832–1920*. New York: Oxford University Press.

Greimas, A. J., & Courtés, J. (1982). *Semiotics and language: An analytical dictionary*. Bloomington: Indiana University Press.

Gumbrecht, H. U. (Ed.). (1988). *Materialität der Kommunikation*. Suhrkamp: Frankfurt am Main.

Humboldt, W. (1988). *On language*. Cambridge: Cambridge University Press.

Jakobson, R. (1990). *On language*. Cambridge, MA: Harvard University Press.

Jameson, F. (1974). *The prison-house of language: A critical account of structuralism and Russian formalism*. Princeton, NJ: Princeton University Press.

Jameson, F. (1997). Marxism and dualism in Deleuze. *South Atlantic Quarterly, 96*(3), 393–416.

Jameson, F. (2002). *The political unconscious: Narrative as a socially symbolic act*. London: Routledge.

Jameson, F. (2008). *The ideologies of Theory*. London: Verso.

Kittler, F. A. (1988). Signal-Rausch-Abstand. In H. U. Gumbrecht (Ed.), *Materialität der Kommunikation* (pp. 342–359). Frankfurt am Main: Suhrkamp.

Kittler, F. A. (1990). *Discourse networks 1800/1900*. Stanford, CA: Stanford University Press.

Krämer, S. (2001). *Sprache, Sprechakt, Kommunikation: Sprachtheoretische Positionen des 20. Jahrhunderts, Frankfurt: Suhrkamp*.

Kristeva, J. (1980). *Desire in language: A semiotic approach to literature and art*. New York: Columbia University Press.

Kristeva, J., & Menke, A. M. (1989). *Language, the unknown: An initiation into linguistics*. New York: Columbia University Press.

Lacan, J. (1991). *The seminar of Jacques Lacan*. New York: W.W. Norton & Company.

Lacan, J., & Fink, B. (2006). *Ecrits*. New York: W.W. Norton & Co.

Latour, B. (1988). A relativistic account of Einstein relativity. *Social Studies of Science, 18*(1), 3–44.

Leclercle, J.-J. (2006). *A Marxist philosophy of language*. Boston, MA: Brill.

Lévi-Strauss, C. (1951). Language and the analysis of social laws. *American Anthropologist, 53*(2), 155–163.

Lévi-Strauss, C. (1963). *Structural anthropology*. New York: Basic Books.

Lévi-Strauss, C. (1966). *The savage mind*. London: Weidenfeld & Nicolson.

Marx, K., & Engels, F. (1965). *The German ideology*. London: Lawrence & Wishart.

McLuhan, M. (1994). *Understanding media: The extensions of man. With assistance of Lewis H. Lapham.* Cambridge, MA: MIT Press.

Michaels, W. B. (2004). *The shape of the signifier: 1967 to the end of history.* Princeton, NJ: Princeton University.

Nietzsche, F. W. (2009). *Writings from the early notebooks.* Cambridge: Cambridge University Press.

Noys, B. (2015, October 27). Matter against materialism. Bruno Latour and the turn to objects. University of Warwick. Retrieved November 2, 2016, from https://www.academia.edu/21686931/Matter_against_Materialism_Bruno_Latour_and_the_Turn_to_Objects

Pasternak, B. (1959). *Doctor Zhivago.* London: Collins & Harvill Press.

Pêcheux, M. (1982). *Language, semantics and ideology: Stating the obvious.* Macmillan: London.

Poster, M. (1982). Foucault and history. *Social Research, 49*(1), 116–142.

Ricœur, P. (1973). The model of the text: Meaningful action considered as a text. *New Literary History, 5*(1), 91.

Ricœur, P. (1992). *Oneself as another.* Chicago: University of Chicago Press.

Rorty, R. (1992). *The linguistic turn. Essays in philosophical method: With two retrospective essays.* Chicago: University of Chicago Press.

Silverman, D., & Torode, B. (1980). *The material word: Some theories of language and its limits.* London, Boston: Routledge & Paul.

Stalin, I. V. (1972). *Marxism and the problems of linguistics.* Peking: Foreign Language Press.

Vološinov, V. (1973). *Marxism and the philosophy of language.* London: Seminar Press.

Wittgenstein, L. (2001). *Tractatus logico-philosophicus.* London: Routledge.

Žižek, S. (1998). The Cartesian subject versus the Cartesian theater. In S. Žižek (Ed.), *Cogito and the unconscious* (pp. 247–274). Durham, NC: Duke University Press.

CHAPTER 6

Material Semiotics
and the Rhizomatic Subject

Abstract This chapter introduces key features of actor-network theory and approaches in its vicinity that together can be called material semiotics. In material semiotics the subject as well as materiality are seen as relational effects. After discussing the methodological suspension of dichotomies and presenting the language of material semiotics as inspired by narrative theory and the semiotics of Greimas, the author introduces a 'materiality of materialization' and presents the subject of material semiotics as an effect of rhizomatic material assemblages. As such, the subject can be understood as a black box.

Keywords Actor-network theory • Latour • New materialism • Subject • Materiality • Semiotics

MATERIAL SEMIOTICS

In material semiotics both the subject and materiality are seen as *relational effects* of situated practices that form what is sometimes called 'actor-networks.' We saw how the subject is decentered in language and in its relation to material conditions. Now, it is also *situationally* decentered in relation to material entities it forms networks with. What is more, in the approaches we will be concerned with now, *materiality* itself is equally

© The Author(s) 2016
J. Beetz, *Materiality and Subject in Marxism, (Post-)Structuralism, and Material Semiotics*, DOI 10.1057/978-1-137-59837-0_6

decentered. Most commonly, the name given to the family of texts and authors studying the emergence of such networks is *actor-network theory* (ANT). The reading suggested in the following allows the empirical and theoretical work of authors such as Michel Callon, John Law, and Bruno Latour to be described by the more general term of '*material semiotics.*'

In this chapter actor-network theory will be presented as *one* form of material semiotics. This immediately broadens our scope by including writers such as Donna Haraway and Annemarie Mol (who cannot be identified with actor-network theory in a strict sense) and solves certain problems associated with the former designation, i.e. ANT. Latour himself once wrote that 'there are four things that do not work with actor-network theory; the word actor, the word network, the word theory and the hyphen' (Latour 1999a, p. 15); so we can feel justified in obliterating that name. Indeed, Latour's approach is not so much a coherent *theory* as it is a methodology and a set of tools for the empirical study of the social. Also, the use of both *actor* and *network* in the theory's name is easily misleading, considering the specific meaning those terms assume in ANT. Denoting it as *material semiotics*, on the other hand, highlights two important aspects of actor-network theory and the approaches discussed in the following chapter. First, talking of *material* semiotics indicates the acknowledgment of material entities in the conception of the social. Second, that it is a material *semiotics* calls attention to a sensitivity for the fundamental *relationality* of the entities studied.

In the present context material semiotics can be understood as 'an empirical version of post-structuralism' (Law 2009, p. 145). Latour, in particular, draws heavily on post-structuralist semiotics, especially those of Greimas,[1] which he regards as 'the organon, as a sort of tool box' (Latour 2006) to treat questions of agency and follow the careers of material objects. Deleuze and Guattari are another point of reference for material semiotics within post-structuralism. Their concept of *assemblage* is closely related to what the term *actor-network* designates (cf. Deleuze and Guattari 1987, p. 4; Law 2009, pp. 145–146). Both Michael Lynch as well as Latour think the name *actant rhizome ontology* would better capture ANT's program (cf. Latour 1999a, p. 19). Material semiotics should not, however, be viewed as a simple transcoding of semiotic and post-structuralist theory into material elements. Such a transcoding is easy enough—Latour writes that 'a semiotics of things is easy, one simply has to drop the meaning bit from semiotics…' (Latour 1996b, p. 375)—but there is more to this approach, which can be characterized by presenting a few key features.

Most of the texts which can be counted as belonging to material semiotics are empirical case studies. The (1) *empiricity* of material semiotics is derived from an insistence on observation and a focus on situated practices. In this respect, it is very similar to *ethnomethodology* with which it also shares (2) an interest in the *productive*, i.e. *performative* properties of those practices. While other empirically and ethnographically oriented social sciences try to *explain* the phenomena in question, (3) material-semiotic approaches are more descriptive and attempt to answer questions of *how* entities come into being in processes marked by material heterogeneity and contingency. What separates material semiotics from ethnomethodological studies is a sensitivity for (4) the *materiality* of realities and relations. Material elements are included in the description of the emergence of associations and are deemed to be a precondition of the relative durability of social realities. At the same time, (5) all *elements* included in these descriptions, be they artifacts, humans, strategies, authority, etc. are treated as *relational effects* of materially heterogeneous 'networks' (or assemblages, or associations), which are themselves products of *processes*. The fundamental *relationality* of all entities implies that they should be analyzed as *semiotic effects*, which entails (6) a suspension of 'classical' dichotomies (subject/object, material/immaterial, macro/micro, nature/culture, human/non-human, etc.) and a dismissal of reifications ('society,' 'capitalism,' 'patriarchy' etc.). While social phenomena and the ordering of reality in dichotomous categories might be the *outcome* of processes, they do not serve as a starting point or an *explanans*—instead they are considered to be the *explanandum*. (7) Describing processes, practices and relations in this manner is achieved through *narrative instruments* that allow the scholar to tell the stories of how human and non-human entities form networks (or fail to do so). Using vocabulary borrowed from narrative theory makes it possible to describe material 'objects' in the same terms as human 'subjects'—as actors or actants that follow programs of action and form associations with other entities. The homology of the descriptive vocabulary helps prolong the omission of dichotomous categories like active/passive, human/non-human, subject/object as these categories are neither assumed prior to the description nor inscribed into the language used. The (8) anti- or non-humanism of material semiotics is the final characteristic of this approach we will consider. The initial indifference to forms of *subjectivity* or the difference between human and non-human as well as the dispersal of agency between heterogeneous actants and actors leaves no room for human essences or anthropocentric reasoning. In Law's words, 'actor-network theory may be understood as a *semiotics of materiality*' which holds that 'entities take their form and acquire their attributes as a result of their relations with other entities' (Law and Hassard 1999, pp. 3–4)—none of which have inherent qualities. Thus, like all entities, human subjects are relational effects. In order to follow the processes in which entities acquire their attributes (or identity), material semioticians employ semiotic tools that allow them to observe 'practices usually subsumed under the names of "power", "institution", and "domination", as well as others such as "instruments" and "equations" which are thought to pertain to cognition' (Latour 1988, p. 9). By regarding human entities as effects and using semiotic tools to report processes without assuming human agency and subjectivity, material semiotics need not 'consider the actor as a subject endowed with some primeval interiority,' but enable the researcher rather 'to observe empirically how an anonymous and generic body is made to be a person' (Latour 2005, p. 208).

An investigation into the relation between, and relationality of, materiality and the subject in material semiotics should begin with a discussion of the methodological repeal of ontological divisions. If, initially, no distinction is made between subject and object, humans and non-humans, immaterial and material entities, and if the ascription of agency is preliminarily held back, this will have consequences for the notions of materiality and the subject. Our first step, then, will be to present the dissolution of classical dichotomies in material semiotics, thereby setting the foundation for a brief discussion of the concepts of actants and actors. This will in turn enable us to introduce *programs of action* in which actors (or that which takes the place of the subject) are *decentered* in associations with other entities. The decentering presented here concerns the subject as the center and origin of actions as well as the subject as the source of *initiatives* and *strategies*. Explicating material semiotics's understanding of materiality will consist of the exposition of materialities' multiple, relational, and processual character.

THE SUSPENSION OF DICHOTOMIES

Material semiotics *suspends* dualisms such as that of subject and object. This suspension can be regarded as a consequence of the assumed relationality of all entities. If everything is a relational effect, then the characteristics of elements are not *essential* and given *a priori* but can be studied in their emergence from heterogeneous material assemblages. As Callon and Law put it, entities 'aren't solid. They aren't discrete, or clearly separated from their context. They do not have well-established boundaries. They aren't, as the jargon puts it, distinct subjects and objects. Instead they are sets of relations, for instance in the form of networks. And they are co-extensive with those networks' (Callon and Law 1997, p. 170).

Because this applies to virtually all entities, dichotomous categorizations necessarily appear as essentialisms which fail to capture the processual, relational, and contingent nature of the elements classified. The principal divisions affected by the methodological dismissal of binary oppositions are those of human/non-human, material/social, material/immaterial, nature/culture, subject/object, technology/society.[2] The distinctions listed are themselves not readily apparent but rather overlap, inform, and enforce each other.

The foundational dichotomy of subject and object, for instance, is not sustainable in a material-semiotic framework because it 'start[s] with essences' (Latour 1999b, p. 180). It is assumed that there is an active part and a passive part, a knowing entity and a known entity, a center of action and a passive object of action. The prior distinction of subject and object often locates the source of agency with the subject and thereby 'prevents the understanding of collectives' (ibid.)—which are not comprised of distinct, definite entities that could be classified independently of their respective collective. Thus, this distinction obscures the view of what is really going on. If the active entity is decided upon beforehand—in other words, if we determine the hero of the story at the outset—there will be no surprises. What is discovered is what was already known. Perhaps what was initially designated the status of the subject *actually* plays the active part, and the object remains passive throughout the processes under scrutiny—a prospect which is highly unlikely.

Designating this outcome as *highly unlikely* reflects the twofold structure constituting the dismissal of foundational dichotomies. One argument for the suspension of the subject–object distinction is *methodological*, while the other could be called *ontological*. Methodologically, the presumption of a subject–object divide is problematic as it restricts the description of processes and practices by determining the *dramatis personæ* prior to the actual commencement of action. Writing about the disadvantages of the 'subject–object fairy tale,' Latour makes the criticism that it 'distributed activity and passivity in such a way that whatever was taken by one was lost to the other' and that 'there were, by necessity, *only two* ontological species: nature and mind' (Latour 1999b, pp. 146–147). Thus, the endowment with 'agency' or activity of anything other than an autonomous human subject was never really *thinkable* in the first place.

The ontological argument insists that all entities should be treated as relational effects. That is to say, it claims that subjects *and* objects 'depend on a flood of entities allowing them to exist' (Latour 2005, p. 208). The argument is *ontological* because it takes the relationality and contingency of entities to be inscribed in the nature of reality. What is *real*—which entities are allowed to share the *ontic* realm with us—depends on their emergence in relational networks. No thing is *autochthonous*—neither are subjects Greek autochthones, born from earth, nor are objects *just there* waiting to be classified by the ethnographer (like 'autochthonic' tribes, untouched by the outside world). The ontology of semiotic relational materialism, then, helps us to 'realize that the world we live in is a mixture' (Mol 2002, p. 31)—a mixture of composite beings continuously in flux.

Both arguments align to support the assumption that 'there are no fundamental distinctions in principle between different classes of entities' (Law and Mol 1995, p. 278). This assumption does not lead to the absence of difference between the entities studied—a philosopher and a stone are not the same thing, and an empirical investigation is likely to reveal some differences between them. Neither does this assumption lead to a universal endowment of 'things' with agency, vitality, or some abstract life force. Ontological differences should not be taken as a starting point, however. Rather, material semiotics begins with a strong suspicion that 'everything is or might be, the same in kind. Everything is, or might be, assembled in a network. And everything is, or might be, dissolved' (Law and Mol 1995, p. 278). The distinction of subject and object, like the other divisions previously mentioned, is thereby *suspended*. It is *suspended* rather than abolished or denied because subjects and objects might return as relational *effects*. Such subjects will hardly resemble the transcendental subject of idealism. What is born from relations in rhizomatic networks in the Deleuzian sense are never *pure* subjects or objects but compound entities. Subjects and objects, in the classical sense, are then merely 'two poles of a spectrum' (Mol 2002, p. 31) with numerous hybrid beings between them. Semioticians of materiality assign various names to the composites located between the poles of subject and object discovered. John Law calls them *monsters*, including himself in this category: 'we are *all* monsters, outrageous and heterogeneous collages' (Law 1991, p. 18). Donna Haraway's concept of *cyborgs* similarly alludes to entities that are neither pure subjects nor pure objects. Latour, in *We Have Never Been Modern*, refers to them as *hybrids* (Latour 1993b) or, following Michel Serres, *quasi-objects* and *quasi-subjects* (cf. Serres 1982, pp. 224ff; Latour 1993b, p. 64). These designations always point to the fact that there are no stable, predetermined entities which can be subjected to an *a priori* categorization. Withholding categorizations like subject/object, human/ non-human, micro/macro as long as possible calls for a special vocabulary able to (linguistically) treat everything *in the same terms*—as we will see in a moment. For now, we can examine the empirical foundation of the theoretical claims made by material semiotics as well as provide a brief example, which illustrates the homogeneous treatment of 'micro' and 'macro' actors.

Material semiotics (especially the version called *actor-network theory*) is less a theory than it is a set of tools, 'sensibilities and methods of analysis that treat everything in the social and natural worlds as a continuously generated effect of the webs of relations within which they are located' (Law 2009, p. 141). The empirical orientation of material semiotics proscribes convoluted theoretical frameworks into which empirical material would have to be inserted and retrospectively adjusted. Whatever theoretical claims are made are (or should be) grounded in empirical studies. Inseparable as theory and practice may be, this descriptive imperative allegedly shields the researcher from a theoretical overload. To give a somewhat odd metaphor, we can imagine material semiotics using empirical reality as a washing machine. Subjecting old entities like 'subject' and 'object' to a hot wash will leave them cleansed of all the dust that has been settling on them for the past two centuries. After this treatment, the two are *suspended*; they are quite literally *left hanging*. When the scientist returns to use, say, the 'subject' again, they will most likely find that it is still somewhat wearable, but has been considerably shrunken and deformed in the process of exposing it to the reality of the washing machine. Also, it might be entangled with the 'object,' making it hard to separate the two once again.

Yet it is evidently possible to write rather abstractly about this approach and describe its theoretical assumptions and ontological underpinnings. This is partly due to material semiotics claiming the possibility of a move to ontological realms in order to answer, albeit cautiously, questions of *what really is*. The difference to 'philosophical' metaphysics is the attempt to answer ontological questions *empirically*, thus instituting an 'empirical philosophy,' (Latour 1993b, p. 72), an 'empirical metaphysics,' (Latour 2005, p. 56) or, as Latour later calls it, an 'experimental metaphysics' (Latour 2004, p. 72), which roots its assumptions about the nature of reality in empirical work.[3]

Suspending the dichotomy of 'micro' and 'macro' can be utilized to illustrate how entities, which are commonly categorized in a specific way, are studied in the same terms. In a text titled *Unscrewing the Big Leviathan* (Latour and Callon 1981), Bruno Latour and Michel Callon argue that all actors should be treated as *isomorphic*. They aim to account for the apparent existence of 'macro-actors' while rejecting the common 'acceptance as a given fact that actors can be of different or equal size' (Latour and Callon 1981, p. 280). But if all actors ('institutions,' 'individuals,' 'representatives') are—initially—the same size, what, then, is the Hobbesian *Leviathan*? It is an actor that speaks and acts in the name of others. Instead of taking this quality as a given, qualifying the Leviathan as a macro-actor, Latour and Callon attempt to retrace the processes which lead to the *emergence* of entities that are more powerful, more influential, 'bigger' than others.

The first requirement for an actor to flourish is the presence of *durable materials*. Authority, influence, etc. can hardly be maintained if they are only produced in situational interactions. Baboons, for example, are *social* animals with *social* skills and hierarchies; yet they never endeavor to construct a Leviathan. If a 'leader' exists, they must *interactively* accomplish this position in situations of bodily co-presence. When the alpha-male turns his back, his authority wanes. In order to recognize who is leading the group, the primates have to constantly observe their surroundings; 'all the actors are co-present and engage in face to face actions whose dynamic depends continually on the reaction of others' (Latour 1996c, p. 229). Social assemblages, which rest their relative durability solely on co-present *bodies* that must continually produce, repair, renew all social relations *in interactions*, are sufficient for baboons (and, according to Latour, for ethnomethodological investigation (ibid.)). For human societies, co-present bodies alone are not enough to build durable assemblies and what are called 'macro-actors.' What is needed are associations *'that last longer than the interactions that formed them'* (Latour and Callon 1981, p. 282) as well as materials that provide solidity and durability. The baboon-king might be able to reign through direct physical intimidation; the human sovereign depends on 'the palace from which he speaks, the well-equipped armies that surround him, the scribes and the recording equipment that serve him' (ibid., p. 284). *Things*, like guns and walls, may make the sovereign formidable, but an actor will have to mobilize additional resources to develop into a 'macro-actor.' They *grow* by solidifying relationships, which in a baboon-society had to be more or less constantly negotiated in face-to-face situations. In Callon and Latour's terminology, relationships which do not require repeated negotiation are placed into a *black box*. A black box generally contains 'that which no longer needs to be reconsidered, those things whose contents have become a matter of indifference. The more elements one can place in black boxes—modes of thoughts, habits, forces and objects—the broader the construction [of the actor] one can raise' (Latour and Callon 1981, p. 283) and the bigger the actor can become. The isomorphism of all actors can still be retained; differences in their relative size are an *effect* of black-boxing—the more durable elements and relations can be put into black boxes, the more 'macro' the actor becomes. To construct black boxes, make relationships durable, assemble an array of materials under oneself, is no easy task. Others have to be interested, their wills translated to coincide with one's own, and the translations need to be fixed by 'reifying [them] in such a way that none of them can desire anything else any longer' (Latour and Callon 1981, p. 296). All actors, big and small, are the result of relatively successful translations and black-boxings *within* a relational network shared with other entities.

In another text written by Callon and Law, a similar definition of black boxes along with a slightly different perspective on the issue of 'micro' and 'macro' actors is presented. In *After the Individual in Society* (Callon and Law 1997), they discuss the relation between individual and collective actors. While they agree that 'micro' as well as 'macro' actors are the effects of processes and that they are essentially *isomorphic*, they add a few interesting aspects. Both individuals and collectives are described as *networks* or sets of relations that are co-extensive with these networks. Furthermore, all actors are understood to be both individuals and collectives.

Callon and Law suspend the difference between the person and the network of entities on which it acts, or, which amounts to the same, 'between the person and the network of entities which acts through the person. Network and person: they are co-extensive' (ibid., p. 169). An example of such an actor—both network and individual—is Louis Pasteur. Bruno Latour, in *The Pasteurization of France* (Latour 1993a) describes how Pasteur became Pasteur-the-great-scientist. He was an *individual*, but simultaneously, he depended on a whole network of entities (including cows, laboratories, other scientists, newspapers, microbes) without which he would not have existed as Pasteur-the-great-scientist at all. Latour's as well as Callon and Law's assertion is that 'Pasteur was a network,' that he was 'nothing more than a network of heterogeneous elements' (Callon and Law 1997, p. 169). He was able to assemble various entities and networks behind himself and made them speak for him, represented them, translated his interests into their language so as to enroll them in his program. Pasteur became a durable, powerful actor because he was able to black-box relations, ways of thinking, ways of speaking, etc. in a way that allowed him to mobilize the relevant actors and networks in his interest. If he black-boxed this whole network of heterogeneous materials and did not exist outside of this network, the metaphor of the black box is transformed. Now, it seems, the actor does not sit atop a black box, but *is* the black box. The claim is 'that a network which is relatively stabilized also tends to become an entity, a black box, a black box that… translates the various materials that make it up' (ibid., p. 174).

Callon and Law further argue that all entities are simultaneously individuals and collectives. An entity which has become relatively stabilized by black-boxing can be seen as a *point* rather than a network. There is no problem with talking about Pasteur as an individual person. If we made the effort of opening the black box to reveal his network, we would find that he can also be described as a collective of diverse entities and networks without which he would not have been able to *act* or be attributed characteristics pertaining to him as a scientist.

The suspension of the dichotomies just described has obvious implications for both the concepts of materiality and the subject. Inanimate material entities can, for instance, not be understood as invariably passive objects. Neither can they be seen as univocally determining instances that human actors are faced with, in the forms of 'nature' or 'technology.' Nor do artifacts that figure in the descriptions appear as enchanted by some 'vibrant matter' that constitutes them. This criticism of reductionist materialism is something Marxism and material semiotics share. The dissolution of the subject/object and human/non-human binaries, however, has consequences for the *acting* subject that are novel to our context. Descartes's self-consciously thinking subject was dismissed in

Marxist thinking and replaced by an ideological subject; the speaking subject expressing itself was decentered in material language. Now, it seems the human subject as the point from which actions and practices originate dissolves in networks without centers where no entity can be assumed to act alone.

The subject is *materially* decentered and disseminated, in such a way that not only its acts but also its characteristics are derivatives of processes distributed among heterogeneous assemblages of hybrids. We will now turn to the question of how material semiotics conceptualizes and describes entities that are usually understood to be human *subjects* or agents, on the one hand, or inanimate objects on the other hand, without reifying the suspended dichotomies. After the concepts of *actant* and *actor* are introduced, *programs of action* will be presented as a tool to describe how entities act, strategize, delegate and share activities, and translate their interests. This will give us a better understanding of the decentering of the subject and lead us to the conception of *materiality* in material semiotics.

The Language of Material Semiotics

The binary concepts criticized by material semiotics are imprinted in language. Describing practices and processes without relapsing into a vocabulary which reintroduces the dichotomies of human/non-human, subject/object, or material/immaterial thus seems almost impossible. One point central to this problem is the description of entities without linguistically presupposing whether they are active, passive, human, singular, or multiple. Another point is the ascription of agency, or better, the localization of origins of action. Here, the approach we are dealing with tells *stories* about how assemblages form or disintegrate without deciding beforehand who is allowed to make a difference.

The language it uses reflects an indifference to static categories by adopting vocabulary from (post-)structuralist theories. This is particularly true for Latour and Law, who borrow their semiotic tools for storytelling from narrative theories. Most notably, Latour's concepts of *actants*, the *programs of action,* and the *trials of strength* are derived from Greimas's structural linguistics and narrative theory. Greimas's narratology generalizes narrative structures of myth proposed by Vladimir Propp as the basic structure of narration. Latour, leaning on Greimas, then uses the narrative theory to develop his *infra-language*, used in the description of actor-networks. While the narrative theory is part of Greimas's rigorous theoretical apparatus that studies language as a system (as *langue*), it is also a tool that enables him to study language as a *process* (cf. Hostaker 2005, p. 8). He proposes a theory of language which encompasses both the paradigmatic and syntagmatic axis. On the syntagmatic axis, language as process is analyzed as narrative. The models generated from the extraction of universal principles of narratives then can not only be utilized for the analysis of manifested language, but can also 'be used to describe social practices' (Greimas 1989, p. 543). Analyzing social practices with models developed in the study of fictional writing gives the semiotician of the material certain advantages. For Latour, what counts most is the freedom of agency that comes with an observation language informed by literary studies. It is literature 'that allows you to give agency to the technical artifact' (Latour 2006). And this is why 'ANT has borrowed from narrative theories, not all of their arguments and jargon to be sure, but their freedom of movement' (Latour 2005, p. 55). When Law writes that material semiotics tells 'stories about how relations assemble or don't' (Law 2009, p. 141), or Latour defines a good descriptive account as 'a narrative… where all the actors do something and don't just sit there' (Latour 2005, p. 128), they refer to narratives where both humans and non-humans can appear as actants or actors, which are defined by their relationality and never act alone.

Actors, Actants, Hybrids, Rhizomes: But No Subjects

Entities are included in the descriptions of processes only if and when they become relevant and *make a difference*. In the accounts of material semiotics, those entities are usually called *actors*. Sometimes, as in Latour's stories, actors are distinguished from *actants*. *Actor* and *actant* are categories established by Greimas for the structural analysis of narratives. Drawing on early structuralists' interpretations of folk tales and myths, the notion of actants offers an inventory of classes of entities in a narrative that are defined by their relations to one another. In fact, their enumeration starts with the Subject and the Object of the narrative, which appears to reapply the suspended categories. But there are also the Sender, the Receiver, the Opponent, and the Helper, and all of them are defined by their relations to another.[4]

As narrative units, these actants can be filled with life by the actors in the story. These 'human or personified' *actors* are the characters, or objects, or animals, which 'accomplish tasks, undergo tests, reach goals' in a narrative (Greimas 1987, p. 70). Greimas distinguishes between actants, 'having to do with narrative syntax,' and *actors*, which are 'recognizable in the particular discourse in which they are manifested' (Greimas 1987, p. 106). Simplifying, we can say that actors are the things in a narrative that have names (Marie, the King, Excalibur) and actants are the narrative units they manifest.

What is important is that actors as well as actants do not have to be human or 'real' as long as they can be identified as 'that which accomplishes or undergoes an act' (Schleifer 1987, p. 88). Law has a very similar view on actors when he writes: 'Humans may, but need not be, actors; and actors may, but need not be, humans' (Law and Mol 1995, p. 277). Another crucial advantage of this terminology is that actants can be manifested by several actors and that one actor can manifest several actants. The number of elements constituting the actant or actor are not determined by the terminology. Used in this way, *actors* can be collective, individual, or both. Neither Latour, nor Callon, nor Law subscribes to the structuralist formalism that lurks behind the terms as they were intended to be used. Mostly, *actor* is used to name entities that make a difference in the story told by scholars in the field of material semiotics.

Latour gives several definitions of actants and actors. In *A Summary of a Convenient Vocabulary for the Semiotics of Human and Nonhuman Assemblies*, written with Madeleine Akrich, an actant is defined as 'whatever acts or shifts actions' and an actor as 'an actant endowed with a character (usually anthropomorphic)' (Akrich and Latour 1992, p. 259). A very similar definition can be found in *Where are the Missing Masses?*, where he uses 'actant to mean anything that acts and actor to mean what is made the source of an action' (Latour 2009, p. 177). In *Unscrewing the Big Leviathan*, an actor is defined as any 'element which bends space around itself, makes other elements dependent upon itself and translates their will into a language of its own' (Latour and Callon 1981, p. 286). In *Science in Action* whatever or whoever is represented is an actant (Latour 1987, p. 84), and in *Reassembling the Social* actors are defined by making a difference and actants are actors that have no figuration yet (Latour 2005, p. 71)—figuration meaning some flesh and features, however vague (ibid., p. 53). However, in *Pandora's Hope* the focus is shifted away from what an actor is, to the question of how it emerges and is defined by a list of trials in which the performance of the entity decides on its fate as an actor. The term actant is only used sometimes, 'to include non-humans' in the definition (Latour 1999b, p. 303). In *The Pasteurization of France* the distinction between actants and actors disappears completely, and the entry in the glossary reads: 'I use *actor*, *agent*, or *actant* without making any assumptions about who they may be and what properties they are endowed with' (Latour 1993a, p. 252).

Such a lax and inconsistent use of the vocabulary lets Latour's adaption of the concept appear as a creative remodeling at best. Latour sometimes uses the terms synonymously, changes their meaning from text to text and never explicitly refers to the actantial categories of Subject/ Object/Sender/Receiver/Helper/Opponent. He might sometimes refer to 'heroes' in his accounts and even frame his stories in a mythical way when writing about those heroes 'triumphing over all powers of darkness' or being challenged by 'a new bad guy, a storm, a devil, a curse, a dragon' (Latour 1987, p. 54), but the categories stay implicit.

Some aspects are, despite all this, kept constant in the accounts of material semiotics. Actants and actors can be human and non-human, and they are actants only if they make a difference. Also, actants and actors—as in Greimas—never act or even exist alone. Both Latour and Greimas treat 'actants as entirely relational and not allowing an essential nuclear core in them to withdraw behind relations' (Harman 2009, p. 156). Actors and actants gain strength through associations with other actors. What is taken from Greimas is the ability to write descriptions, which let act whatever acts and show relations in their making, without assuming the origins of agency at the outset. The main benefit of Greimas's model, in other words, is that actors, 'both non-human and human, can more freely be constructed on a joint plane of immanence' (Hostaker 2005, p. 6). In empirical reports, one actor can be chosen as the starting point (Pasteur, an object like a door, a company, etc.) and might remain the central figure of the narrative. But the terminology equally allows the writer to depict *rhizomatic* networks as actors without a discernible center. Just like in Deleuze and Guattari, where 'any point of a rhizome can be connected to anything other' (Deleuze and Guattari 1987, p. 7), the *actor*-networks can consist of a multitude of connections and relations that are continuously transformed in observable processes. Both in the ontology of material semiotics and in that of Deleuze and Guattari, this 'multiplicity has neither subject nor object, only determinations, magnitudes, and dimensions that cannot increase in number without the multiplicity changing in nature' (Deleuze and Guattari 1987, p. 8).

The methodological–ontological focus on relationality and heterogeneous assemblages is thus expressed through the use of semiotic vocabulary, which enables the researcher to *think* and describe entities as multiple, singular, active, passive, subject, object all at once without changing the terminology. *Subjects*, dependent on the assemblages from which they emerge as actors, lose their wholeness and unity as soon as they are described in this way. It follows that 'no human subject is merely a human subject—all are more or less durable, more or less extended networks' (Boyne 2001, p. 25); they are quasi-subjects—at best.

How, then, is directed action possible? Is it not true that *humans* drive cars, shoot guns, write books, or embark on missions like 'consciously producing their material life'? The dispersal of agency and the distribution of action among different actants and actors can be illustrated by presenting *programs of action* as a tool of empirical description.

Programs of Action: Decentering the Subject Some More

If an actor has a goal, an intention, something it might do or something it is in a (whatever vague) way supposed to do, we can speak of a *program of action* (cf. Latour 1999b, p. 178). Such a program of action is always a trial, a struggle, against anti-actors with their anti-programs, which try to prevent the actor from fulfilling their program. The *pasteurization of France*, for example, could be described as the program of action Pasteur followed in Latour's book. Another prominent instance of a program of action is the introduction and conservation of scallops in St Brieuc Bay, described by Michel Callon in his text *Some Elements of a Sociology of Translation* (Callon 1986). Each time, actors have to defeat anti-programs, take detours to complete another program first, delegate tasks to others, or build associations with a heterogeneous mix of actors/actants to reach their goals.

These programs of action are a generalization of Greimas's narrative programs (cf. Akrich and Latour 1992, p. 260). In a narrative, a program is 'composed of an utterance of doing governing an utterance of state' and can be interpreted 'as a change of state effected by any subject (S1) affecting any subject (S2)' (Greimas and Courtés 1982, p. 245). A subject does something affecting them/itself or something/someone else. With such a minimal definition, there is a multitude of programs present in even the most boring story. 'The monkey ate an apple' would have a narrative program because the monkey changes a state (before the eating) by a doing (eating the apple) into another state (after eating the apple).

But what if the apple is hanging from a tree and the primate has to obtain it before it can enjoy it? It will have to run an *instrumental program*. This can be done in several ways. It can fetch a stick in order to get the apple it wants to eat. Or it can throw a stone or shake the tree. If it is a clever monkey, it can also delegate the task of obtaining the apple to another actant. It can manipulate a member of its group into getting it, or—even more clever—work a machine that does it. This delegated instrumental program is called an *annex program*. The first program can be called a *base narrative program* to distinguish it from the two others (cf. ibid.). In a novel, where the reader follows a heroine and her programs (together they form the *trajectory* of the story), there will be trials and obstacles to overcome. There will be anti-heroes and anti-programs. That means, 'in a more or less hidden way' the 'story of the villain' is told as well (ibid., p. 205), while the starting-point and the trajectory followed (whose story is told and when it starts) is decided for the reader.

When settings and processes are studied with material-semiotic instruments, however, the starting point has to be chosen by the researcher, who also decides whose story will be told. Once a starting point is picked, we can follow the actors in their *programs of action*. In the observation language we are concerned with, there are no instrumental or annex programs, yet there are *detours* and *delegations* (cf. Latour 1999b, p. 174; Latour 1995, p. 278), which denote something similar. And another crucial instrument is added: *associations* with other actors. We already said that actors form networks, assemblages, and associations and that each of them is always an actor *within* such networks. We can now add that associations can be *instrumental*. When, however, the other associated actors change the original program of action, and do not just act as *intermediaries*, those actors become *mediators*.

Mediators can be material instruments or objects just as much as human beings—the differences are, as we know by now, suspended. If, for example, someone is betrayed or hurt and wants to take revenge (that is their program of action) they might not be strong enough to avenge themself when facing the enemy empty handed. They must make a detour to reach their goal. So the person forms an association with another actant: a gun (a gung-ho friend would be another option). If the original program of action had been 'shoot the enemy!' and they went on to do so with the gun, that gun would serve as an intermediary (cf. Latour 1999b, p. 178), as a simple instrument that does not make a difference in the achievement of the end. Most of the time, according to Latour, something else is the case. Out of the association between gun and person, a new actor emerges ('citizen-gun, gun-citizen' (ibid., p. 179)), and the program changes. It is not the program of the person, nor the program (script) of the gun. It is something new. 'You only wanted to injure, but now with the gun in your hand, you want to kill... and the gun is different with you holding it' (ibid.). There is a hybrid actor, and it is not possible to attribute the action of shooting to either the gun or the person. Being betrayed and hurt are properties rarely ascribed to sticks and stones. Furthermore, it is possible to state that an actor wants to take revenge. These are all statements, which *momentarily* seem to *center* the actor described. It is an entity that has properties and characteristics. Yet, as soon as we move on to *how* a planned action is achieved, we find the actors entangled in a miscellany of beings which partake in the action. So programs are fulfilled by *associating* with other actors or actants which may have programs of their own, and thereby translate and transform the original programs. And if we pick, as a starting point, an actor and their program, we may find that the actor is not one single (non-)human being but a network, a hybrid that does not act alone and does not have a program of their own.

There is more to programs of action deserving of our attention. Take the program of a lone concierge of an apartment building in Berlin: 'Please lock the door behind you during the night and never during the day' (Latour 2000, p. 17). If he wants everyone to do as he wishes, he will have to bring the inhabitants of the house on his side. He can do so by telling everyone in person what a nuisance it is to constantly have to check whether the door is locked or not. He would have to associate with the inhabitants, but in some way could still be described as the sole actor from which the program flows. If he chose to put up signs saying 'please lock the door behind you during the night' his program would be delegated to something else. Achieving such an ambitious goal with just a few words or a sign is unrealistic if we consider the masses of anti-programs it faces. Thieves, lovers, doctors, mailmen, dogs all want to enter the building during times it is supposed to be shut. The concierge has to counteract all those anti-programs. In Latour's story—the story of the Berlin key—the concierge forms associations with a key, the door and a Prussian locksmith (ibid., p. 18) to fight the disobedient Berliners. The new key's *script materializes* a program of action by making sure that tenants lock the door behind themselves when entering the building during the night. It has two identical bits on each end, and to retrieve the key after unlocking the door, it has to be pushed through the key-hole and turned again on the other side of the door, thereby locking it again. During the day this mechanism is disabled by the concierge—the doors cannot be locked. Who is acting now? Is the key the agent behind the program?

On the one hand, the material key *transforms* a program of action, which was thus far only present in the sign and the words of the concierge, into an object. We go from the world of signification to the world of things. On the other hand, the key does not just *express* the same semiotic content in another form. Then it would simply be an intermediary; it would merely 'carry, transport, shift, incarnate, express, reify, objectify, reflect, the meaning of the phrase: "Lock the door behind you during the night, and never during the day"' (Latour 2000, p. 18). The key is a mediator because it *forms* and *makes* the disciplinary relations necessary for the program to be successful, and does not solely express them (cf. ibid., p. 20 ff.).

The key, however, would not work by itself. That is to say, it does not exist in the way it does *in and of itself* but only in relation to the tenants, the door, and the concierge. If the inhabitants of the house found a way to render the door mechanism useless, the key would lose its characteristic of *making a difference* in the story told. Equally, if the door was broken, or the concierge stopped disabling the mechanism in the morning, not only would the program not be fulfilled, but the key would lose its significance. The person with the gun, the concierge with the locksmith, the door, the key—none of them act alone. They only act and *exist* in associations or networks. They are constituted in associations and thus a result of the relations they are part of. 'Objects, entities, actors, processes—all are semiotic effects: network nodes are sets of relations; or they are sets of relations between relations' (Law and Mol 1995, p. 277).

There are no monadic autonomous actors manipulating their material environment by unilaterally forcing their will on the entities they manipulate. Their will, their strategies, their plans are never completely unaffected by the other entities they associate with. Paraphrasing Marx, we could say: 'The actors make their own networks, but they do not make them just as they please in circumstances they choose for themselves; rather, they make them in situations that are materially heterogeneous and contingent,' If there *is* a subject, it does not act alone of its free will. The actants, actors, entities or hybrids the actor shares responsibility and agency with can certainly be *material*. Guns, machines, scallops, keys are all *things* possessing some sort of materiality. But being a *material* entity is, as it turns out, a relational effect like everything else. Whether an entity is material or not cannot be decided a priori.

RELATIONAL MATERIALISM AND THE MATERIALITY
OF MATERIALIZATION

Materiality is an effect of relationality and is *produced* in practices. Therefore it is nothing stable and unchanging. Like all characteristics of entities which enter the descriptions of material semiotics, the materiality of an element is not assumed at the outset. Only by observing the complex processes at work in a particular setting can *material* things be made visible as 'the relationally variable effects of practices,' which means that accounts of material-semiotic approaches 'talk more of mattering and materializing than of matter and materiality' (Law 2010, p. 187). Material semiotics is not so much concerned with 'things' or 'matter.' Matter is not given any metaphysical essential properties like 'vitality' or 'vibrance.' This orientation towards the malleability of materiality rather than its ontological fixity also distances these approaches from such reductionist materialist theories that characterize materiality as the 'efficiency and stubbornness of matter, imprinting chains of cause and effect onto malleable humans' (Latour 1999b, p. 190). To juxtapose material semiotics from reductionist materialism, like neo-Darwinism, cognitivism, materialisms of matter, and static conceptions of materiality, its empirical philosophy can be called *relational materialism*. That materiality is not static—as the materialists he criticizes hold—but relational, and in certain ways *produced*, leads Latour to claim that matter and materiality, as it is usually understood, 'is not a given but a recent historical creation' (Latour 1999b, p. 207).

Conceiving of materiality as produced, enacted, relational and processual does not make it any less *real*. One of the core claims of the parts of material semiotics that are sometimes called Science and Technology Studies or laboratory studies is that 'whatever emerges from an experiment is an *effect* of the relations that are assembled and held together in it. Natural, social, and human materials and realities, *all* of these are understood as effects rather than causes' (Law 2010, p. 178). To become material, an entity has to *matter*, that is, it has to make or be made to make a difference. *Making a difference* means, at once, to be real and to be detectable. In Latour's *Science in Action* (Latour 1987), an entity's materiality and reality is determined in *trials of strength*. An actant has to pass trials which decide how *real* it is by testing its resistance. In his *Irreductions*, he writes: 'Whatever resists trials is real' (Latour 1993a, p. 158).

An entity can become less material, less real, or vanish all together if it fails tests. Latour gives the example of N-rays, which were 'discovered' by a French physicist. They were recognized, papers were published on them, and they seemed to resist trials. It was only when an American scientist decided to visit the physicists' laboratory and put the N-rays through new ordeals, that they lost their competences, their essence. Upon the removal of an aluminum prism that was supposed to measure the rays' performance, and the discovery that that the results (inscriptions on metal plates) were still the same, the N-rays lost all their materiality. The inscriptions were made by something else. There were no N-rays anymore (cf. Latour 1987, pp. 75f).

The claim deduced from observations in laboratories is ontologized by material semiotics by supposing that 'realities only exist in the practices that materialize them' (Law 2010, p. 180). Not unlike the 'things' in Marxian theory that cannot be abstracted from practical human activity, such realities exist only in practices. Thereby, the dualism of materiality/immateriality is methodologically suspended in the same way as the other dichotomies are suppressed. In *Unscrewing the Big Leviathan* discussed earlier, Latour and Callon write that '[t]here are of course macro-actors and micro-actors' (Latour and Callon 1981, p. 280), only to then argue for an indifference to this fact in order to observe *how* actors grow to be macro-actors. By the same token it is possible to discard the assumption that certain entities are material.

In *empirical scientific* practice it is possible to maintain that only what makes a difference is real and material, simply because entities which do not *change* anything will not even appear in the observation. No researcher would deny that the stone they are holding in their hand is material—because in that moment *it makes a difference*. Entities like the Higgs boson, however, have to be *materialized* in the situated practices of experimental physicists at CERN. The particle has to resist trials, be detectable, enter relations with other particles, machines, scientists, etc. to *become* material. Its materiality was practically accomplished in 2012—but how stable and durable it is depends on its resistance in future trials. Someday it might share the realm of immateriality with the ether, N-Rays, and Zeus. The same could be said about the recently detected gravitational waves. This is one way in which Law's assertion in *The Materials of STS* can and should be understood. He writes: 'Matter that does not make a difference does not matter. It is not matter since there *is* no relation. No relation of difference and detection. No relation at all' (Law 2010, p. 173).

As soon as an entity makes a difference it automatically stands in heterogeneous material relations with other entities. The inverse is also true:

as soon as an entity stands in heterogeneous relations with other entities it makes a difference and is material. No thing ever acts or exists alone. The relations are not heterogeneous simply because a multitude of human and non-human entities assemble in them. There is also a heterogeneity of qualitatively different *materialities*. A variety of gradations of *durability* and *resistance*—all of which derive their properties from relational processes—emerge and change in the respective assemblages described. The materiality of the Berlin key changes when the mechanism of the door is disabled by the tenants; just like the durability of a prison wall can only be assessed in the relations it might be forced to enter with the wit of the inmates, tied-together bed sheets, or explosives. Durability and resistivity are, then, not a *given* but a relational effect. Similarly to what we encountered in Marxist materialism, to be *material* means to be real (resist trials and make a difference) and to obtain a certain durability which is the *product* of miscellaneous relations marked by alliances, delegations, conflicts, struggles and so on. It is for this reason—the relationality and processuality of *networks*—'that the world is a kind of kaleidoscope in which materiality is continually being organized and reorganised' (Law and Mol 1995, p. 286).

It was said that material semiotics has a sensitivity for the materiality of social processes and relations. Material entities are seen as a condition for the relative durability of the social, which—without its material support—would be dependent solely on interactions performing the social relations of a collective. Materiality and sociality are thus regarded as co-extensive. Social dynamics exert their force by the inclusion of materials which outlast the situation of their original appearance. What is designated as *property relations* in Marxist theories, for instance, procures its stability not just from repeated situated negotiations between actors, but is made durable by material instances like walls, armed police forces, prison buildings, courts, but also ideological practice and many other things. How strong and resilient (i.e. real and material) these instances are at a given juncture is, for material semiotics, exclusively assessable by observing the practices and processes which *materialize* them. If their materiality is undermined by counter-programs, they lose their permanence.

The Great Wall of China might be said to be less material today than it was 1000 years ago. Apart from corrosion and heavy machinery causing its decay, counter-programs materialized in tunnels as well as airplanes advanced the de-materialization of the wall by subverting its power to separate geographical areas. For two actors who wish to kiss each other but are separated by the wall, on the other hand, its materiality is as stable and durable as it can be. What this illustrates is that, just like in Saussurean semiotics where signifiers and signifieds are only *significant* in their relationality, *materiality* is a relational effect.

In material semiotics, materiality is thought to be a complex matter. The multitude of materialities assembles under the modalities of what could be called (1) *relational materiality*. Because the relations in heterogeneous assemblages are not fixed but in flux, the modality of (2) *processual materiality* or alternatively that of *a materiality of materialization* should be added. All the other modalities of materiality we encountered in the preceding chapters can thus be understood as *effects* of relational processes of *materialization*. Thus, the *positive materiality of matter* is an effect. Objects, for example, cannot be seen as isolated objects of passive contemplation or determining forces abstracted from practices. The modality of the *materiality of effectivity* or *objectivity* is here understood as an effect of relations and processes that have some kind of durability, make a difference, and 'matter.'

THE SUBJECT AS EFFECT OF RHIZOMATIC MATERIAL ASSEMBLAGES

What such a designation of materiality entails for the conception of the subject in material semiotics remains to be determined. Thus far, what could be shown is that entities—human beings included—are not assigned to categories like *subject, macro,* or *active* before the fact. Furthermore, actors form alliances and associations and *can* be, but do not have to be, described as co-extensive with the networks they form and are a part of. The empirically vested ontological claim about all entities, then, is that they do not act alone and are always *effects* or nodal points of relationally configured networks of miscellaneous entities.

One way to conceptualize human subjects from this perspective is to simply deny their existence altogether. This can happen by refusing to work with the categories of subject and object or by omitting the distinction between human and non-human. What would follow is a metalanguage of description, which would be not only far removed from how human actors experience reality but also scarcely readable. The idealist metaphysical claim of the existence of a unified primary subject would thereby simply be traded in for the equally strong and ontological assertion that nothing resembling a subject can ever exist. Material semiotics assumes neither the absence nor the presence of subjects or objects, but methodologically *suspends* these categories and ontologically argues against an essentialism that insists on the primacy, originality, and autonomy of the subject.

Another way to look at human actors is to resist the temptation of taking the dichotomy of subject and object for granted and retracing how entities come into existence. Approaching 'subjects' in this manner entails deconstructing them and describing them as networks without a predetermined center or as effects of materially heterogeneous assemblages. The subject (if there happens to be one) can thus be described in its emergence. This difference between *denying* the subject and methodologically *suspending* it at the beginning of an observation is crucial here. Denying the possibility of (experienced or apparent) subjectivity presumes characteristics and thus restricts the description as much as reifying the subject at the outset. Following processes and practices while at once retaining a sensitivity for *materializations* and refraining from strong assumptions about the realities observed affords a method of description which safeguards the researcher against distorted accounts. This is what the approach of material semiotics *does*. The subject then appears as 'more social, fabricated, and collective than hard nature,' and its only 'essence' is 'change, alliance and hybridity' (Boyne 2001, pp. 29–30). It is an unstable result of rhizomatic material configurations in flux.

It seems impossible to *talk* and *think* about human subjects in this way without constantly explicating the networks that constitute them. A statement like 'Pasteur discovered microbial fermentation' would be inadmissible because it reifies Pasteur as a subject and fails to present him as the materially diverse network he really is. But material semiotics never describes *all* processes and networks that figure in a specific setting. This simply means leaving some *black boxes* shut. *Names* are shortcuts, black boxes, conventions. It is possible to say 'Einstein' while being conscious of the fact that he was not a single point, an autonomous subject, but a *network* of scientists, books, equations, institutions, newspapers, bodies and so on. In the same vein, it is possible to say 'capitalism' without reifying it as an entity that exists outside of all the innumerable entities, processes, practices, and relations which constitute it.

The individual subject is a *black box*. It *exists* and can be spoken about, but if we choose to open the black box to see what constitutes it and how it came to be, the *material* rhizomatic network, outside of which the subject has no reality, can be made visible. When material semiotics pick a human entity like Pasteur as a starting point, the 'object of the study is not so much to celebrate as to deconstruct the subject' by *showing* that it 'is an effect, a product of a set of alliances, of heterogeneous materials' (Law 1991, p. 12). This is what Latour means when he writes that '[f]ull-fledged human subjects and respectable objects out there in the world cannot be my starting point; they may be my point of arrival' (Latour 1999b, p. 182). Leaving all the black boxes closed would institute subjects as something they are not: centered, homogenous, autonomous entities that only rely on themselves. The project of material semiotics 'has precisely been to decenter the heroic subject' (Law 1991, p. 12) by means of empirical studies.

The black box of the subject is filled with the relationships, entities, alliances, objects etc. which are not in need of constant re-actualization and negotiation. Like Pasteur or the Leviathan, the black-boxed network of the subject can extend and grow; or, like *Aramis*, the train system (cf. Latour 1996a) and the network of St Brieuc Bay (cf. Callon 1986) shrink and disintegrate into new forms (cf. Boyne 2001, p. 30). The more durable entities and relations that can be black-boxed, the more durable and 'successful' the subject is in the programs of action followed in a narrative. The durability and stability of each network is reliant on *material entities* that obtain their gradations of *materiality* in relation to other entities. The size and the success (power/dominance/authority) of human actors (or subjects) can therefore be described as an *effect* of relational processes of *materialization*.

NOTES

1. Latour writes 'it would be fairly accurate to describe ANT as being half Garfinkel and half Greimas' (Latour 2005, p. 54, n. 54).
2. We could add: 'meaning and materiality, big and small' (Law 2009, p. 147), 'material and social' (cf. Latour 2005, pp. 75–76), 'words and world, society and nature, mind and matter' (Latour 1999b, p. 267), 'person and network' (Callon and Law 1997, p. 169), 'human/animal' (Latour and Callon 1981, p. 284), 'human action and material causality' (Latour 2005, p. 85), or Haraway's 'troubling dualisms' of 'self/other, mind/body, culture/nature, male/female, civilized/primitive, reality/appearance, whole/part, agent/resource, maker/made, active/passive, right/wrong, truth/illusion, total/partial, God/man' (Haraway 2004, p. 35).

3. In Harman's characterization, Latour 'always insists that we cannot philosophize from raw first principles but must follow objects in action and describe what we see. Empirical studies are more important for him than for almost any other philosopher' (Harman 2009, p. 14).

4. For scientific probity's sake, we should note that Greimas concept of actants of a narrative owes a great deal to Propp's dramatis personæ, which consists of the villain, the donor, the helper, the sought-for person (and her father), the dispatcher, the hero and the false hero (cf. Greimas 1983, p. 201). Terry Eagleton puts it nicely when he writes, in *Literary Studies*: 'A. J. Greimas's *Sémantique structurale*, finding Propp's scheme still too empirical, is able to abstract his account even further by the concept of an actant, which is neither a specific narrative even nor a character but a structural unit. The six actants of Subject and Object, Sender and Receiver, Helper and Opponent can subsume Propp's various spheres of action and make for an even more elegant simplicity' (Eagleton 1996, p. 91).

REFERENCES

Akrich, M., & Latour, B. (1992). A summary of a convenient vocabulary for the semiotics of human and nonhuman assemblies. In W. E. Bijker & J. Law (Eds.), *Shaping technology/building society: Studies in sociotechnical change* (pp. 259–265). Cambridge, MA: MIT Press.

Boyne, R. (2001). *Subject, society, and culture*. London: Sage.

Callon, M. (1986). Some elements of a sociology of translation: Domestication of the scallops and the fishermen of St. Brieuc Bay. In J. Law (Ed.), *Power, action, and belief: A new sociology of knowledge?* (pp. 196–223). London, Boston: Routledge & Paul.

Callon, M., & Law, J. (1997). After the individual in society: Lessons on collectivity from science technology and society. *The Canadian Journal of Sociology/ Cahiers canadiens de sociologie, 22*(2), 165–182.

Deleuze, G., & Guattari, F. (1987). *A thousand plateaus: Capitalism and schizophrenia*. Minneapolis: University of Minnesota Press.

Eagleton, T. (1996). *Literary theory: An introduction*. Minneapolis, MN: University of Minnesota Press.

Greimas, A. J. (1983). *Structural semantics: An attempt at a method*. Lincoln: University of Nebraska Press.

Greimas, A. J. (1987). *On meaning: Selected writings in semiotic theory*. Minneapolis: University of Minnesota Press.

Greimas, A. J. (1989). On meaning. *New Literary History, 20*(3), 539–550.

Greimas, A. J., & Courtés, J. (1982). *Semiotics and language: An analytical dictionary*. Bloomington: Indiana University Press.

Haraway, D. J. (2004). *The Haraway reader*. New York: Routledge.

Harman, G. (2009). *Prince of networks: Bruno Latour and metaphysics.* Prahran, VIC: re.press.

Hostaker, R. (2005). Latour—Semiotics and science studies. *Science Studies, 18*(2), 2–25.

Latour, B. (1987). *Science in action: How to follow scientists and engineers through society.* Cambridge, MA: Harvard University Press.

Latour, B. (1988). A relativistic account of Einstein's relativity. *Social Studies of Science, 18*(1), 3–44.

Latour, B. (1993a). *The pasteurization of France.* Cambridge, MA: Harvard University Press.

Latour, B. (1993b). *We have never been modern.* Cambridge, MA: Harvard University Press.

Latour, B. (1995). Gaston, a little known successor of Daedalus. A door must be either open or shut: A little philosophy of techniques. In A. Feenberg & A. Hannay (Eds.), *Technology and the politics of knowledge* (pp. 272–282). Bloomington: Indiana University Press.

Latour, B. (1996a). *Aramis, or, the love of technology.* Cambridge, MA: Harvard University Press.

Latour, B. (1996b). On actor-network theory: A few clarifications plus more than a few complications. *Soziale Welt, 47,* 369–381.

Latour, B. (1996c). On interobjectivity. *Mind, Culture, and Activity, 3*(4), 228–245.

Latour, B. (1999a). On recalling ANT. In J. Law & J. Hassard (Eds.), *Actor network theory and after* (pp. 15–25). Oxford: Blackwell.

Latour, B. (1999b). *Pandora's hope: Essays on the reality of science studies.* Cambridge, MA: Harvard University Press.

Latour, B. (2000). The Berlin key or how to do things with words. In P. Graves-Brown (Ed.), *Matter, materiality, and modern culture* (pp. 10–21). London: Routledge.

Latour, B. (2004). *Politics of nature: How to bring the sciences into democracy.* Cambridge, MA: Harvard University Press.

Latour, B. (2005). *Reassembling the social: An introduction to actor-network-theory.* Oxford: Oxford University Press.

Latour, B. (2006). Where constant experiments have been provided. A conversation with Bruno Latour. St. Louis: Arch Literary Journal.

Latour, B. (2009). Where are the missing masses? The sociology of a few mundane artifacts. In D. G. Johnson & J. M. Wetmore (Eds.), *Technology and society: Building our sociotechnical future* (pp. 151–180). Cambridge, MA: MIT Press.

Latour, B., & Callon, M. (1981). Unscrewing the big Leviathan: How actors macro-structure reality and how sociologists help them to do so. In K. Knorr-Cetina & A. V. Cicourel (Eds.), *Advances in social theory and methodology:*

Toward an integration of micro- and macro-sociologies (pp. 277–303). Boston: Routledge & Paul.

Law, J. (Ed.). (1991). *A sociology of monsters: Essays on power, technology, and domination.* London: Routledge.

Law, J. (2009). Actor network theory and material semiotics. In B. S. Turner (Ed.), *The new Blackwell companion to social theory* (pp. 141–158). Chichester: Wiley-Blackwell.

Law, J. (2010). The materials of STS. In D. Hicks & M. C. Beaudry (Eds.), *The Oxford handbook of material culture studies* (pp. 173–188). Oxford: Oxford University Press.

Law, J., & Hassard, J. (Eds.). (1999). *Actor network theory and after.* Oxford: Blackwell.

Law, J., & Mol, A. (1995). Notes on materiality and sociality. *The Sociological Review, 43,* 274–294.

Mol, A. (2002). *The body multiple: Ontology in medical practice.* Durham, NC: Duke University Press.

Schleifer, R. (1987). *A. J. Greimas and the nature of meaning: Linguistics, semiotics and discourse theory.* London & Sydney: Croom Helm.

Serres, M. (1982). *The parasite.* Baltimore: Johns Hopkins University Press.

CHAPTER 7

Conclusion

Abstract The social world is fundamentally material. This materiality consists of much more than just matter or matter in motion. Material conditions, social relations, processes, practices, thought, discourse, associations, etc. are all material and can be subsumed under different modalities of materiality. The subject is constituted by and in material instances. It is the effect of conditions, relations, processes, and practices within these different materialities. A non-reductionist theory of the subject must acknowledge the materiality of the social.

Keywords Materiality • Subject • Materialism • Marxism • (Post-) Structuralism • Material semiotics

There is not much left, it seems, of the ideational realm that took primacy over the material in idealist ontologies. Their immaterial ideas, universal principles, and eternal essences have taken the yellowed patina of the books they first appeared in. With each step of our investigation, the realm of the immaterial shrank further and made the early materialist inversion of idealism, which still retained the binary of 'material' and 'immaterial,' less viable.

In *Postmodernism. Or, the Cultural Logic of Late Capitalism,* Jameson writes that '[c]apitalism, and the modern age, is a period in which... the deep underlying materiality of all things has finally risen dripping and convulsive into the light of day' (Jameson 1991, p. 67). Recognizing this

© The Author(s) 2016   137
J. Beetz, *Materiality and Subject in Marxism, (Post-)Structuralism, and Material Semiotics,* DOI 10.1057/978-1-137-59837-0_7

fundamental materiality and claiming that the social world is and always *was* material, does not amount to proposing that everything is just matter.

Marxism, (post-)structuralism, and material semiotics have in common that they conceive of materiality as multiple and complex, or, in other words, not reducible to tangible solid matter or matter in motion. The materialities encountered in our investigation were assigned to different modalities of materiality. In our discussion of Marxism, three such modalities could be identified, all of which were subsumed under the negative definition of *not being ideal.* The *positive materiality of matter* was characterized as encompassing such tangible entities as bodies and artifacts as well as phenomena like spoken language and weather. This modality most closely resembles the reductionist materialist understanding of materiality. In Marxist theory, however, such materialities of matter cannot be understood as abstracted from human activity. It is never just matter that constitutes this form of being material. The second modality introduced was designated as a *materiality of displacement* or *mutability,* which included processes and practices as material phenomena. This intangible materiality was described as deriving its material character from the fact that it changes and transforms aspects of the material world. The third kind of materiality implicit in Marxist thinking was named the *materiality of objectivity* or *effectivity,* denoting (in)tangible materials such as social relations, rules, institutions, etc. which exert an objective force on individuals.

The modalities identified in Marxist theory could then also be applied to the multiple materiality of language and discourse. In this context the *positive materiality of matter* consisted of sound waves, bodily gestures, and inscriptions on surfaces, which all comprise matter in the form of particles, atoms, molecules, or waves. But again, this materiality of language cannot be abstracted from (signifying) practices, and the practical activities of speaking, writing, reading, understanding, thinking individuals. What was called *materiality of displacement* or *mutability* referred to the processual and practical dimension of language and discourse. As in Marxism, the *materiality of effectivity* was ascribed to 'rules' (of language) and the diverse number of institutions encountered in this chapter.

The gradations of materiality set forth by material semiotics in addition to the previous types were subsumed under the overlapping modalities of *relational materiality* and the *materiality of materialization.* While the former was meant to highlight the relationality of all entities and their being construed as relational effects in this approach, the latter pointed to the processual character of the relations in which entities materialize. The emphasis on practical activity shared by the three approaches allow for the claim that materiality is not a given, objective category but multiple and the result of processes and practices.

Furthermore, none of the theories presented adhere to the dichotomy of materiality and immateriality. In the readings suggested above, this dichotomy is suspended in material semiotics, disabled by the absence of the ideational from the conception of reality in Marxist theory, and disposed of in (post-)structuralism on account of thought never being outside of language. Indeed, what could that 'immaterial' be after language, thought, beliefs, relations, ideology, and so forth were all presented as belonging to different modalities of materiality?

The groups of theories and methodologies chosen for our survey further share the notion that what has been called the subject should be regarded as an *effect*, rather than a starting point or origin. In each, the subject is at once constituted and decentered in and by material instances. It could be shown that in neither material semiotics nor Marxism nor (post-)structuralism is there a temporal succession in which an individual is constituted as a subject or a unified subject is decentered by material conditions, discourse, or assemblages. In Althusser's theory of ideology the individual interpellated as subject is always-already a subject. Equally, in (post-)structuralist approaches the subject does not enter discourse to then be decentered by it; rather in order to be constituted as a subject the individual has to already be in language, which simultaneously decenters it. Material semiotics conceives of the subject as a black box which is the result of relational processes of materialization.

All theories outlined in the preceding chapters refute a concept of the subject which posits the latter as pure *hypokmeímenon*—foundation and origin. The subject is always an effect or a result of material processes, practices, or relations. The converse designation of the subject—as *subiectus*, i.e. subordinate, subjected—is equally unsatisfying, however. The material processes, practices, and relations which were presented as the decisive instances in the subjects' constitution do not exist independently of the subjects and their interactions; they are no outside force which unilaterally subordinates subjects. The social and the material are co-extensive.

From a position that sees the subject as an effect of material instances we can paint a dire portrait of what is left of the autonomous, unified subject. As an ideological subject, it is always-already caught up in ideology and conditioned by the material conditions it finds itself in; as a speaking subject, it speaks as much as it is spoken by language and is the effect of discursive practices; as the result of heterogeneous associations, it is never the unified center of action. The subject today appears as fissured and decentered, its unconscious colonized by commodification and its relations to other subjects reified. But we should not fall into the trap of an unwarranted (idealist) universalization of the *form* subjectivity takes in our times. Maintaining that the subject is an effect of social conditions, relations, discourses, and processes entails the—at its core historicizing—notion that in different material conditions and social relations other subjectivities have obviously existed and are possible.

In Chap. 4 a possible criticism of Althusser's theory of ideology was voiced when it was said that universalizing the category of the subject runs the risk of underrating the specificity of the subject in capitalism. This is true for other theories of the subject as well. When speaking of a subject decentered by social forces, discourse, or associations, the specificity of the material conditions, the forms discourses take, and the associations possible at one particular juncture should always be acknowledged. There is evidently no hope to return to an autonomous subject that never existed—one that is the sole origin of action and meaning, free from social conditioning and not even partly constituted in language. But we can hope that in different material conditions that do not resemble late capitalism and its horrors, it might be possible to see new subjectivities emerge which are not conditioned by social relations of exploitation, discourses marked by inequality and dominance, and commodification as well as the other forms ideology takes in our present mode of production.

We end our investigation here. In its brevity it did not develop a comprehensive theory of the subject or a non-reductionist materialism. We have, however, developed a number of characteristics of the mechanisms that constitute the subject in material instances and were able to delineate the central forms materiality takes, thereby setting the foundations for a materialist approach to the subject. Such a non-reductionist materialist theory of the subject takes its departure from a modest claim: Outside of the manifold materialities there exists—nothing. †

REFERENCE

Jameson, F. (1991). *Postmodernism, or, the cultural logic of late capitalism*. London: Verso.

INDEX

© The Author(s) 2016   141
J. Beetz, *Materiality and Subject in Marxism, (Post-)Structuralism,
and Material Semiotics*, DOI 10.1057/978-1-137-59837-0

Printed by Printforce, the Netherlands